POLICE HORSES

by

JUDITH CAMPBELL

1971 EDITION

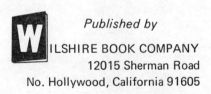

Published by
WILSHIRE BOOK COMPANY
12015 Sherman Road
No. Hollywood, California 91605

Printed by
HAL LEIGHTON PRINTING CO.
P. O. Box 1231
Beverly Hills, California 90213
Telephone: (213) 276-4794

POLICE HORSES. © Judith Campbell, 1967. First American edition published 1968 by A. S. Barnes and Company, Inc., Cranbury, New Jersey 08512.

Library of Congress Catalogue Card Number: 68-29876

6943
Printed in the United States of America

CONTENTS

	List of Illustrations	7
1.	'Proper Persuers' to Mounted Police	11
2.	The Making of a Police Horse	33
3.	No Duty comes Amiss	54
4.	Around Britain	68
5.	Duty Amongst the Skyscrapers	81
6.	Iranian Stallions and the Desert Patrol	94
7.	Australian Trooper Police Horses	106
8.	Policing the Canadian Plains	129
9.	Around the World	148
10.	Police-Horse 'Characters'	167
	Index	181

5

1892 Los Angeles Police Department Paddy Wagon Last Used in 1904 by San Pedro Division

LIST OF ILLUSTRATIONS

Page

'The Man on the White Horse'. Lt-Colonel Sir Percy
Laurie and Quicksilver — 17

London's mounted 'Peelers', 1860 — 17

Police horses involved with suffragettes, 1914 — 18

Moving along the 'Reds', 1925 — 18

Traffic control in Paris, between the wars — 35

Policing Paris in 1920 — 35

Warrior, an ex-cavalry charger — 36

Australian Trooper Police, 1880 — 36

Trooping the Colour, 1967. The Queen riding Neill — 45

Leading the cortège at Sir Winston Churchill's funeral — 46

City of London police horses — 47

The occasional slip-up — 47

Helping the public — 48

The new and the old — 48

Imperial, competing at Richmond — 73

Radio telephone in use — 73

Nuisance training — 74

Nuisance training again — 91

Salford police horses on park patrol — 92

Edinburgh horses on crowd control — 92

A Newcastle upon Tyne contingent — 92

Page

Jumbo, the Downs Ranger's horse, Sussex   109

A Kingston upon Hull policeman and horse   109

A Royal Canadian Mounted Policeman at work   110

Two members of Jamaica's Mounted Branch   110

New York mounted police at work after dark   127

Rusty, a Boston police horse   127

From the Garde Républicaine de Paris   128

The Rock, famous show-jumper from Italy's Carabinieri   128

Men and horses from the Carabinieri on duty   145

Stuttgart mounted police   146

A South African policeman and horse   163

Rescuing a floundering swimmer, Holland   163

In Malta   164

Traffic work in Tokyo   164

Officer in charge of New South Wales mounted police   173

Lesotho police on patrol   174

A Bahrein stallion   174

Firing from the saddle, Teheran   175

Bedouin of the Camel Corps   176

Jordanian horses near Jerusalem   176

ACKNOWLEDGMENTS

GRATEFUL thanks are due to the following for permission to use illustrations: Lt-Colonel D. St C. Laurie, OBE, MC, p 17 (top); Syndication International, p 17 (bottom); *Radio Times* Hulton Picture Library, p 18 (top and bottom), p 73 (right); Direction des Services Techniques, p 35 (top and bottom); *Southern Evening Echo*, p 36 (top); Marc Henrie, p 45; London Express News & Feature Services, p 46; C. S. Wilkins, p 47 (bottom); Keystone Press Agency, p 73 (left); Scotsman Publications Ltd, p 74, p 92 (middle); the Canada House Library, p 110 (top); New York Post Corporation, p 127 (top); *Pony/Light Horse*, p 128 (bottom); Godfrey Argent Ltd, p 175, p 176 (top and bottom); and to the police forces of Australia, the City of London, London's Metropolitan District, Edinburgh, Newcastle upon Tyne, Salford, Eastbourne, Kingston upon Hull, Jamaica, Boston USA, Paris (Garde Républicaine), Italy (Carabinieri), Stuttgart, South Africa, the Netherlands, Malta, Tokyo, Lesotho.

CHAPTER ONE

'PROPER PERSUERS' TO MOUNTED POLICE

THE history of the horses of the Mounted Branch of the Metropolitan Police in Great Britain begins in 1758, when 'two Persuit horses and proper Persuers' were attached to the offices in Bow Street belonging to the renowned Fielding brothers.

The law of those days was savage, and public executions and floggings were not only common punishments, but also a popular form of entertainment. More than 200 offences, varying from horse-stealing to pilfering 5s-worth of merchandise, carried the death penalty. Yet despite this code of penal brutality the cities and their environs, and London in particular, still teemed with thieves and vagabonds, harlots and highwaymen, and the householder slept with a loaded blunderbuss to hand.

Governed by freely elected if sometimes corrupt magistrates, guarded by inefficient, underpaid civilian constables and nightwatchmen known as 'Charlies', with only the hated military Redcoats to call on in emergencies, neither the metropolitan area nor Britain at large possessed any organised force for keeping law and order until about the middle of the eighteenth century. Then a stipendiary justice of Westminster, Henry Fielding, the noted author of *Tom Jones*, inaugurated the force which eventually became the famous Bow Street Runners or Thief Takers—a force that was later carried on and extended by John Fielding, Henry's remarkable blind step-brother and co-magistrate.

In the 1760s Sir John Fielding produced a 'Plan for Preventing Robberies within Twenty Miles of London'. A crying need of the time was for foot patrols to operate on winter nights in the fields surrounding London, and also for a regular force of mounted men to watch the turnpikes, and intercept the many criminals attempting to evade capture by crossing the parochial boundaries. This scheme however would involve a greatly increased number of paid officers. The Seven Years' War was ending, and certain that any large reform of the police force would be refused by the Government, Sir John asked for the temporary expedient of a regiment of light horse to be stationed in the metropolitan area. Instead, the First Lord of the Treasury sanctioned a horse patrol of eight men and animals, which incorporated the two original mounted 'Persuers'.

Although there were turnpikes within a couple of miles of Charing Cross the area involved was a large one; yet this little patrol was an acknowledged success. Even so the experiment was discontinued when less than two years old. The decision came from Government level, and from then on there was no regular Bow Street Horse Patrol until it was begun again forty years later, under the auspices of the chief magistrate, Sir Richard Ford.

Sir John Fielding could certainly have done with his trained mounted men to complement a Warning to Travellers, Stage Coachmen and Others that he issued in 1767. It concerned 'that Gang of unhappy wretches', living in idleness and subsisting on plunder, who were making it their particular business 'to cut off Trunks from behind Post Chaises, to steal Goods out of Waggons, from the Baskets of Stage Coaches, Boots of Hackney Carriages, and out of Carts which carry Goods to and from Inns. . . .'

There were also the highwaymen. The ancient method of raising the hue and cry was by horn and voice, and at a later stage it was suggested that mounted patrols be 'furnished with a horn the sounding of which will alarm the neighbourhood and make it difficult for the offenders to escape'. In 1775 there was no mounted patrol, with or without a horn, to prevent tragedies such as the one that occurred in Epping Forest, when seven highwaymen waylaid the Norwich coach and killed the guard, though not before that resourceful man had shot dead three of his assailants.

The regular Bow Street Horse Patrol was begun in 1805 to provide patrols for all main roads up to a distance of 20 miles from Bow Street. It had a provisional strength of fifty-two men and animals, their numbers varying according to the annual fluctuations in the price of fodder. The men, all ex-cavalry, over thirty-five and married, were paid 28s a week and housed in cottages close by the roads they patrolled. As a safeguard against the pilfering of horse feed, the patrolmen's wives were forbidden to keep pigs or poultry. The men each carried sabre, pistol, truncheon and a pair of handcuffs. Their scarlet waistcoats, worn with blue greatcoats and trousers, black leather hats and stocks, white leather gloves and steel-spurred Wellington boots, quickly earned them the obvious nickname of Redbreasts. They were a brave sight in their colourful uniform, the first to be issued to any British police force, and in an age when the horse was supreme the Redbreasts, however few in numbers, proved invaluable. Indeed they were so successful in protecting travellers on the main roads that when the Bow Street patrol area was restricted in 1821, the Horse Patrol was actually increased in numbers.

It was an era when Stubbs was painting his pointed-headed, sinew-quartered equine aristocrats; when 25,000 rural shoeing-smiths were kept fully employed, not to mention those plying their trade in the towns; when anyone sufficiently affluent to dispense with his own legs for travelling, rode behind or on a horse, and the pace of life in general, and of traffic in particular, was starting to speed up. Though as late as 1789 some of the country highways in winter became so bogged with mud as to be impassable even to carts and waggons—and the country gentry again went visiting on horseback, their ladies riding pillion as in days gone by—it was only a little time before Macadam and Telford, that 'Colossus of Roads', would be producing the hard, granite surfaces which made the first good roads in Britain since the Romans constructed their highways centuries before. Mr Obadiah Elliott's patent elliptic springs were making lighter coaches and carriages possible, and the traffic was galloping in and out of London with ever-greater velocity. In 1750 it took two days to travel by coach from London to Bath, yet by the early nineteenth century the journey had been cut to fourteen hours.

To more speed and comfort in travel, greater safety could now be added. By 1820 thousands of the acres of heaths and thickets that had harboured highwaymen had come under the plough, and that particular quarry of the Horse Patrols soon became a menace of the past.

When the reigning Czar visited London in 1814 he commented, interestingly, that he considered it was the lack of an adequate preventive force that made our punishments so ferocious. Fifteen years later, after humanising the penal code, and despite public suspicions of a law that seemed to smell of foreign practices, Robert Peel with his Metropolitan Police Acts gave London its first 'Bobbies', the prototype for a force which gradually spread throughout the country.

By 1813 the control of the Bow Street Horse Patrol had passed from the Chief Magistrate to the Home Secretary. In 1836 the horse patrol was incorporated into Sir Robert Peel's new disciplined unarmed police force, although still retaining its individual status, with separate responsibilities and duties. Three years later the Mounted Branch became an integral part of the Metropolitan Police, proud members of the first effective force for keeping law and order that Britain had known. It became, too, part of the new conception of the police that gradually began to percolate people's minds.

It took time. At first the new guardians of the law were received with taunts and jeers. They were called Blue-bottles, Blue-devils and Unboiled Lobsters. Rude ditties were sung about them round the streets, while the 'Charlies', the ineffectual old watchmen they had replaced, became the undeserving heroes of sentimental verses. When one of the new Bobbies was charged with stealing a leg of mutton, the street urchins were provided with a heavensent opportunity for demanding its return from every man in police uniform who came their way. In 1842, under the newspaper headline of OUTRAGE BY POLICEMAN, was printed the sad story of a young gentleman aged fifteen, who was proceeding quietly on his way towards his home in Islington. The presence of a mob caused him to make a detour, when suddenly 'a cowardly brute mounted on horseback, rode up, and with a blow of his truncheon struck the unoffending individual senseless to the ground'. It is a relief to read that after being kept quietly in bed for two days he was restored to his usual health.

From now on the 'persuit horses' were to be used for more purposes than those of merely chasing and apprehending miscreants. Prevention rather than detention is the first principle of the police forces of today, and eventually Peel's Bobbies came to be viewed in a friendly light by at any rate the majority of the populace, regarded as law keepers whose very existence tended to preserve the peace.

The old Bow Street Horse Patrol would not have been required to deal with crowds or riots. With few exceptions such disturbances remained the province of the military, although the tragedy of Peterloo remained as a raw reminder of what could happen if troops had to be employed on crowd control. In August 1819 50-60,000 people, assembled to petition for the repeal of the Corn Laws, were addressed at a meeting held on St Peter's Field, Manchester. Alarmed by the numbers and by some drilling that had taken place the previous evening, the magistrates ordered the arrest of the speaker. When neither the chief constable nor a detachment of the Manchester & Salford Yeomanry were able to break through the crowd, troops of the 15th Hussars were called on to do the job. They drew their sabres, the crowd panicked, and though the figures given for the resulting casualties vary between eleven killed and 400 injured, to five or six killed and seventy wounded, the whole episode was a horrifying and unnecessary disaster.

On the other hand some force had to control the crowds, if there were not to be repetitions of the Gordon riots when the London mob burned seventy houses and four gaols in 1780. It was to be some years before the new mounted police would replace soldiers in this sphere. There are reports of trouble in Preston when the soldiers fired and killed two rioters; in 1842 Dragoons with drawn swords were assisting the foot police during disturbances in New Cross, Manchester, and the military also fired on a crowd at Blackburn, killing two.

For many years to come the mounted police of London were to be considered of most use as country patrols and, distributed amongst the outer divisions of the metropolitan area, were employed principally in patrolling the main roads. During the Chartist riots however, when unruly mobs thronged inner London claiming a People's Charter, which included demands for universal suffrage, vote by ballot and annual parliaments, the mounted police were mobilised there to retain order. From time to time they were also employed in Hyde Park to regulate the crowds attending public meetings. At a meeting of 5,000 Chartists on Kennington Common, the presence of 800 foot and twelve mounted policemen is noted—a striking comment on the efficacy of police horses for controlling a crowd. Gradually the mounted police took over, and eventually the cavalry were confined to purely military duties. As a result of the West End riots of 1886, it was decided to increase the mounted force for central London and the outer divisions, so that they would be available for any similar outbreaks as well as for regulating large gatherings and processions.

London's mounted Peelers were a more sober-hued lot than their flamboyant Redbreast forerunners. Like the foot police they had blue uniforms, and their tunics were more or less the same as those of today. They wore tall hats, then pill-box caps with chin straps, replaced by helmets in 1865, and an abundance of whiskers, perhaps to counterbalance the hair lacking on their bob-tailed horses. The carrying of firearms was out, truncheons only were the order of the day, and until 1885 they carried a rattle instead of a whistle. But it was not only the uniform and conception of the police force that was changing, the age too was being transformed—and Queen Victoria was on the throne.

The railways, ushering in the epoch of coal and iron, and changing not only the landscape but the scope and tempo of individual living, came with Victoria. Gone for ever was the quiet isolation of the English countryside, as known during and for some time after the rumbustious era of the Regency. For years

'The Man on the White Horse'. Lieut-Colonel Sir Percy Laurie, KCVO, CBE, DSO, Assistant Commissioner of the Metropolitan Police 1919-1936, and his horse Quicksilver

London's mounted 'Peelers' acting as guardians of Derby Day, 1860

Police horses were frequently involved with the suffragettes.
Raid on Buckingham Palace 1914

The horses are always there when trouble is brewing—'Reds'
at Bow Street, 1925

to come the city streets would still resound with the rumble and thunder of iron wheels, the clatter of horses' shoes, and be thronged with horse-drawn omnibuses, hansom cabs and the private broughams and carriages of the wealthy, but the short-lived glory of the stage and mail coaches was over. Never again would the yard of the Bull & Mouth in Piccadilly be a scene of bustle and hustle, as chambermaids and waiters, yard boys and ostlers, jostled to fill a stage coach inside and out with adults and boxes, bundles and children, while the coachman sat aloof fingering his ribbons, and the four horses clattered their hooves in a fever to be off.

The first steam-driven carriages were on the road as early as 1801 and must have given the horses of the Bow Street Patrol food for thought. Thirty years later Peel's mounted sections would be meeting the steam coaches by then plying regularly between London and Brighton. The 'Man and Flag' Act of 1864 killed off these monsters by limiting their speed to four miles an hour, and no doubt the police horses were as relieved as those of the civilians, but already the smell of motor-car was in the air. There were not so many years to go before a gentleman walking in the pleasant environs of Paris found it not uncommon to meet 'a little open vehicle flitting along without apparent means of motion, upon noiseless rubber-shod wheels, or panting forth a gentle warning from a square-shaped box in front'. Before very long that little vehicle and its offspring would have changed the pace and tenor of life beyond recognition. Yet police horses have remained an active component of that transformed world; and by the middle of the twentieth century one of the recognised duties of a mounted policeman has become the untangling of the Gordian knots of vehicles that choke our city streets.

To modern thinking the great Victorian epoch may appear in some ways an age of cant, a symbol of stuffy gentility, but above everything else it was a period of enormous change and reform. The majority of householders gained the vote and, at last, a secret ballot. Working conditions in factories and mines were improved, the penny post made communication by letter a possibility for even the poorest. The Chimney Sweeps Act was a result not only of the public stir caused by Kingsley's book *The Water Babies*, but also of a generally growing awareness of the extent and iniquity of the exploitation of children. Wages rose, working hours shortened, income tax varied between 2d and 6½d in the £, and standards of education, sanitation, health, lighting and locomotion continued to rise. All these events obviously had bearing on the crime of the age. The two factors that probably most affected the police force as a whole were the rapid urbanisation of Britain, and the rise in population by about 15,000,000. Unfortunately the State played small part in urban planning, and the continued and lasting spread of warrens of mean streets and slums provided ample opportunity for mounted street patrols to prove their usefulness in years to come.

During the Victorian era, too, mounted policemen began to become part of scenes of national rejoicing and mourning. In the splendid celebrations for the Queen's Diamond Jubilee, British police horses were joined by a contingent of the Royal Canadian Mounted Police, who crossed the Atlantic to ride in the procession. The relief of Mafeking, where Colonel Baden Powell and his gallant defenders were saved from surrender or death, and from a diet of horse, locusts and mule, in May 1900 brought out the London crowds for two nights of 'wonderfully enthusiastic jubilation, which seemed to effect a complete change in the character of Englishmen and Englishwomen'. Their enthusiasm caused them 'for the nonce, in the general cheering and waving of Union Jacks, to appear the most excitable people on the face of the earth', and it is to be hoped that the horses of the Mounted Branch, out in full force, had been well schooled in 'nuisance training'. Only a year later the horses were on duty at Paddington station when the foreign princes arrived to pay their last respects to the old Queen. They were there, too, amongst the sombre crowds thronging Hyde Park to watch the funeral cortège of a sovereign who, according to Lytton Strachey, retained her 'vitality, conscientiousness, pride and simplicity . . . to the latest hour'. With the death of Queen Victoria a whole age had passed away.

Despite the closing months of the Boer War, despite the largely

ignored rumblings of war to come, the Edwardian scene is chiefly
remembered as an era of gaiety. Under the leadership of the
middle-aged King Edward VII, the upper stratum of fashionable
society was gay enough; and the King's genial character and
natural dignity helped to popularise the Crown in wider circles.
But the mass of the population were earning not more than 20s a
week, and demands for social and political reforms were gaining
momentum. The often large-scale agitations brought problems of
crowd control and breaches of the peace never before encountered by any police force; the specialised training received by
police horses for dealing with recalcitrant humans was to be well
tested.

The militant suffrage movement grew from a Women's Social
& Political Union formed by Mrs Emmeline Pankhurst in
Manchester in 1903, but apart from a few skirmishes, the really
militant part of the campaigning for women's rights did not
start until three years later. This was the time when the suffragettes began to contrive every kind of cunning stratagem to outwit
the police who wished to remove them, appearing here and there
in different disguises, addressing the terrace of the House from
river boats, chaining themselves to railings, popping up anywhere and in any manner that would draw public attention to
their cause. Their so-called 'raids upon Parliament', when a
deputation of women would be chosen from a nearby meeting to
process in orderly fashion towards the House, soon became
regular features of the campaign. Large forces of both foot and
mounted police were used to prevent the suffragettes reaching
Palace Yard, and although at that time they offered no violence
other than attempting to continue towards their objective, the
inevitable crowds following on behind usually caused a scuffle.
When Edward VII died in 1910, the good-hearted, high-
principled King George V inherited the suffragette dilemma
along with labour strikes, the Irish problem, and the first world
war.

It was during this reign that the despatching of messages
became generally entrusted to telephone and cycle, and with
economy in mind a reduction was made in the number of horses

owned by the Metropolitan Mounted Branch. The authorised strength was now 126 horses, with a reserve of twelve kept at the Adam & Eve Mews, Paddington, in the charge of an inspector and a small staff of grooms. Their duties varied from controlling the over exuberance or inexpertise of the horsemen, young ladies, grooms and children who still flocked to ride in Rotten Row, to patrolling common land or breaking up the meetings of unruly strikers in the docks. There were plenty of police horses present at the Derby of 1913, but neither they nor anyone else were able to prevent the fanatical suffragette Emily Davidson from throwing herself to a tragic death beneath the flying hooves of the racehorses. When a deputation headed by Mrs Pankhurst marched on Buckingham Palace to try to see the King and protest against the forcible feeding of imprisoned suffragettes, both foot and mounted police were, as always, embroiled in the mêlée; the infuriated women even tried to drag the police officers off their horses' backs.

In that same year King George and Queen Mary paid a visit to Blackpool, where their mounted police escort was under the command of the youngest chief constable of his day, a fine horseman. Scarcely a year later war was declared, and Blackpool's dozen or so horses, in which this officer took such obvious pride, were reduced to two regular police mounts, groomed and exercised for the duration by a young woman. The world was caught up in a maelstrom, a war in which for the last time horses were to play their full and bloody part.

Throughout the country and in the metropolitan area police horses were still needed for their normal duties, and for those directly connected with the war. They were out on the London streets keeping the peace amongst the eager militant crowds just before the declaration of hostilities with Germany. There were mounted police to keep an eye on the throngs of young men beseiging recruiting offices in Whitehall, all determined not to be left out of Kitchener's New Army of the First Hundred Thousand—fortunately none prophetic enough to see how few would return. The horses were out amongst the throngs in the Strand on Anzac Day in April 1916.

The casualty lists grew ever longer, the youth of the nation was drained, and more and more horses were needed to maintain the armies in France. In Britain there was a compulsory purchase from tradespeople of horses for the army, and inevitably some police horses were shipped across the Channel. In turn, once peace was restored, a number of chargers found their way into the ranks of the mounted police.

One of these ex-army horses was a sixteen-hand grey gelding called Warrior. He served with the Old Contemptibles in France from 1914 until the end of the war, taking part in the retreat from Mons and being wounded in the advance on the Aisne. After an operation to remove shrapnel, he returned to duty and took part in several further actions. He was brought back to England, and after the Armistice was bought by a Southampton lady and presented to the town. Warrior, gentle and intelligent, became the most honoured and beloved of Southampton's police horses. He died in 1935 aged twenty-six years, and one of his hooves was mounted to become the gavel for Southampton's branch of the Old Contemptibles' Association. His story is told on a memorial stone in the Civic Sports Centre.

It is impossible to read any account of the Great War without learning of the many exploits of that outstanding cavalry regiment, the Royal Scots Greys. One of their officers, Lt-Colonel Laurie, became Assistant Commissioner of the Mounted Branch of the Metropolitan Police almost immediately after the war, and was the architect of the fine force of men and horses that London possesses today. In 1915 the Army Remount Department purchased a grey horse in Ireland which was shipped to France in the spring of 1916 and transferred to Colonel Laurie, who christened him Quicksilver. This was the beginning of a partnership that lasted for the next twenty-seven years—until Empire Day in 1943, when Quicksilver, in his thirty-fourth year, was put down in his favourite paddock on Colonel Laurie's estate in Wiltshire.

With his master the grey horse served in France, Belgium and Germany, from February 1916 to March 1919. He was badly wounded at the battle of the Somme, was at the Ypres salient until transferred to the 4th Army headquarters, and in 1918 advanced with the 2nd Army into Germany, crossing the Hohenzollern Bridge at Cologne. Quicksilver was unique amongst horses in being awarded the Mons Star, a wound stripe, the War Ribbons of the Expeditionary Force, the General Service and Victory Ribbons and the Order of the Blue Cross.

During his seventeen years as a police horse, Quicksilver became one of the best-known horses in Great Britain, and to the populace of London Colonel Laurie—knighted in 1933—was always 'the Man on the White Horse'. Until their retirement he and Quicksilver were present at every State opening of Parliament, and all State drives and visits of foreign royalty. They attended the weddings of the Princess Royal and the Duke of York, later King George VI, of the Duke of Kent, who was killed in an aeroplane crash during world war II, and of the Duke of Gloucester.

On 11 November 1918 the mounted police were of course on the London streets in full strength, keeping a friendly eye on the thousands of cheering people bent on celebrating the end of the war to end all wars. The horses had their full of waving flags and dancing, exuberant crowds; of the clanging of bells and shrilling of whistles, and all the delirious relief of a nation once more at peace. The horses were on duty outside Charing Cross when the Duke of Connaught met the French war hero Marshal Foch; they were there again for the triumphant return of Sir Douglas Haig, the British commander-in-chief, and his generals.

War, as always, solved few problems and created a multitude of new ones. In Britain there were those who tried to return to the ways of a world that vanished on the banks of the Somme in 1915; there were others who reckoned Utopia should be at hand. But the post-war years were times of stress and change, of political and social upheaval, with frequent strikes as the visible sign of underlying unrest and injustice. Even some thousands of the Metropolitan and City police came out on strike—action which seems incredible today—in protest at the delay to a promised rise in pay. A year later a few came out again, when a

Parliamentary Bill was passed forbidding policemen to join their
own union. It will be no surprise to horsemen to learn that on
both occasions, whatever the views or actions of its rider, no
police horse was deprived of its normal attention. When Colonel
Laurie became Assistant Commissioner in 1919, he completely
re-organised the Mounted Branch of the Metropolitan Police on
much the same lines as those on which it is run today.

At that time there was a feeling in some quarters in Britain
that the day of the police horse was ending, a point of view that
was to be expressed at intervals for some years. The senior officers
of the mounted police were issued with cars instead of horses and
traps, but otherwise neither the Assistant Commissioner nor the
men under his command were unduly concerned with the
internal combustion engine. Now, almost fifty years later, the
police force is mobilised with fast cars and motor bicycles, 'Panda'
patrols and even experimental helicopters, as an integral part of
the motorised age in which we live. Yet many policemen still
prefer to control a crowd from the back of a steady horse than
in any other way. Vehicles can be overturned, the man on foot
has no great advantage of height or strength, but a mounted
policeman can see across the heads of a crowd to the source of
any possible trouble. He can pick out and talk to the people concerned, and there is always the innate respect, tinged with fear,
in which a horse is held by the majority. The policeman can
ride his horse forwards and know that, nine times out of ten,
the people pushing in the front will control themselves, and those
behind, by stepping back out of the way of the horse's feet. If a
turbulent element should turn unpleasant, the rider of a trained
horse can rely on his mount to put shoulder and chest to good
account, and thrust back trouble makers. In an age of increasing
crime, a mounted patrol is the surest deterrent to attacks on women
and children amongst the heaths and commons outside British
cities, or along the leafy rides of places such as Epping
Forest.

In Holland about 350 foot police used to be needed to safeguard and clear the enormous motor-racing track at Zandvoort.
Since the mounted police took over part of this duty, twenty men

and horses, strategically positioned, have replaced 200 of the men on foot.

In Britain during the twenties, PC Scorey with his grey horse Billy provided the classic example of crowd control by a mounted man. The constable, a native of Bristol, had previously served twenty-one years with the Royal Scots Greys, before following his commanding officer, Lt-Colonel Laurie, into the Mounted Branch of the Metropolitan Police. Billy, Yorkshire-bred, was his first police mount, and the pair became well known as star performers at fêtes and horse shows. On a famous day in 1923 King George V was present at Wembley to watch the first Cup Final. From the royal box he looked down on an enormous crowd of over-excited spectators and rival fans, who began to swarm over and through the turnstiles and barricades despite all efforts by the foot police. Within minutes the playing pitch was completely obliterated, and it appeared that the football match of the year had become an impossibility.

With the police powerless and the air charged with that terrifying emotion generated by an unruly mass of people, it was a moment when a trivial incident could flare up into dangerous scenes. Ten mounted policemen had arrived as reinforcements, but even they could not break their way through to the pitch. Then suddenly an officer on a big grey horse appeared, waving both arms to motion back the surging crowds while he guided his horse with his legs, and rode forwards. No animal is more sensitive to human feeling than a horse, no sound more menacing than the inarticulate roar of a crowd, but Billy, true to his training and completely confident in his rider, never faltered. PC Scorey was able to open up a space where it was possible for his comrades to operate and follow his example. Eventually the King and players reached the pitch unhampered, and Bolton Wanderers and West Ham were able to play on to their historic final.

For ten years PC Scorey and Billy were an inseparable team, on duty together on almost every occasion when great crowds were out in the metropolitan area. They were there for the weddings of King George VI, Princess Mary and Princess Maud, and

were on crowd control at the funeral of Queen Alexandra. Just
after the war they had the task of helping to disperse rioters in
Whitehall, and the constable even met his future wife through
Billy, when she came up to admire and pat the big horse. When
on duty in the East End during the General Strike of 1926, the
pair were recognised : 'Here's the bloke from Wembley !' shouted
a local wit, 'they've sent him to settle the strike like he settled
a football match !' Billy died in December 1930.

Public approval for the mounted police was far from universal.
Letters to the press repeatedly demanded to know why it was
necessary for London to have a purely decorative police force. A
young lady who had watched the force on parade was quoted
as saying, 'How delightful and pretty, but what earthly use are
they ?' The horses were accused of providing an excellent means
for senior police officials to get cheap exercise. They were said to
be ridden in the vicinity of the Mounted Police Training Centre
at Imber Court by young women disporting themselves, with a
police groom in attendance—an interesting comment on the strict
rule, in force for many years now, that no civilian other than Mrs
Archer Houblon, who schools the Queen's mount before Her
Majesty's official Birthday Parade, may ride a police horse. The
police were criticised for spending money on augmenting the
Mounted Branch, and were exhorted to cut out the ornamental
stuff and come down to earth, where householders and shopkeepers were shouting for protection. Police horses were accused
of being a sort of show civilian cavalry, and although it was con-
ceded that they were necessary for controlling crowds, they were
said to be of more hindrance than help in controlling traffic—
a viewpoint which may be recalled with wry incredulity today
by horses and riders toiling in the infinitely thicker traffic snarls
of London and Teheran, Tokyo, Stüttgart and even New York

It was their steady concentration on the work they could do
best which, over the years, vindicated the Mounted Branch of the
Metropolitan Police in the eyes of the sceptics. When crowds
gathered, as happened so frequently in the years between the
wars, they were always required. Soon after the first war, for instance, 10,000 unemployed gathered along the Embankment,

intending to send a deputation to demand a higher scale of Poor
Law relief from the Minister of Health. Their intention was
frustrated and, tempers rising, the procession converged on Hyde
Park, where fortunately the leaders managed to persuade them
that a conflict with the accompanying mounted police would not
further their cause. According to a newspaper report, the police
and their horses were given a good-tempered cheer as they can-
tered away across the Park. Trouble with the unemployed was of
course recurrent. Most of the demonstrations and marches were
orderly, but occasionally irritation mounted. A large crowd that
converged on Whitehall demanding to see Lloyd George was dispersed with the help of mounted police; during a fracas in West
Ham when a constable was injured, a general fight ensued, truncheons were used, and reinforcements of mounted police arrived
at the gallop. There were May Day demonstrations, and when
the 'hunger marchers' of the thirties arrived in London, there was
plenty of work for foot and mounted men in maintaining law and
order.

Earlier when sixty Communists assembled in Trafalgar Square,
and marched to Waterloo Place en route for the German Embassy
in Carlton House Terrace, it was the police horses who drove
them back, two of the officers suffering injuries. In 1925 during
trouble with the 'Reds' at Bow Street, the horses were used to
clear both footway and street. When 10,000 people met in Hyde
Park before marching off to the Japanese Embassy to protest
against Japan's attitude to China, the mounted police were forced
to draw their long baton-truncheons.

During the nine days of the General Strike in 1926, thousands
of 'specials' were enrolled to take over, sometimes with odd results, the normal duties of the police, releasing trained men to deal
with a potentially tricky situation. There is even a record of a
mounted patrol of specials—polo players with their ponies, whose
enthusiasm for keeping law and order was damped by the con-
tents of chamber pots, emptied upon their heads from the upper
windows of houses in a cul-de-sac in Whitechapel. Mounted
police helped materially in maintaining order during the strike.
They had plenty of escort duties, such as conducting a petrol

wagon through Southwark, or accompanying the first tram to
leave New Cross after the strike was over. Partly because of the
insistence by trade-union leaders that no provocation must be
offered, partly because the majority of the strikers were themselves ex-service men, the incidence of violence was surprisingly
small. Stones were thrown, heads were broken, arrests were made;
mounted and foot police charged and broke up crowds in Hull
City Square, and Metropolitan horses were used to clear the
road at the Elephant & Castle after a riot: but by and large and
considering what could have occurred, the strike was an orderly
affair. The police, both mounted and on foot, were looked on
as men with a job to do, and dislike was mostly reserved for the
interloping 'specials'.

Less routine work has come the way of most mounted policemen at one time or another. A mounted constable was com-
mended for his quick judgment when he galloped after the runaway horse of a lady riding in the Row, and forced it into the rails
—only seconds before it would have erupted into the traffic on
Hyde Park Corner. A gentleman who had apparently looked on
the mounted police only as an ornamental force, wrote to *The
Times* to say how impressed he had been by the speed and
expertise with which a mounted officer dealt with a van horse
that fell in the roadway—while the well-trained police horse 'stood
quietly by, all unattended in the roaring traffic, a very pretty
sight indeed'. Mounted police took charge of the situation when
a water main burst in New Cross Road, and a torrent threw up
portions of the roadway, causing traffic chaos. In the Thames
floods of 1928, policemen rode their horses through the water to
rescue people in danger of drowning.

The mounted policemen have had their casualties—an officer
was thrown and killed during the rehearsal for King George VI's
and Queen Elizabeth's wedding—and their ceremonies. In the
thirties Lt-Colonel Laurie took the salute, from the steps of Westminster Cathedral, of a large contingent of his men riding at the
head of the Metropolitan City Catholic Police Guild, after a
requiem mass for their comrades who died in the Great War.

In the days when Britain still possessed an Empire, a vast Em-

pire Thanksgiving was attended by King George and Queen
Mary in Wembley Stadium. In front of the King was drawn
up a solid square of brilliantly uniformed troops, broken by
one avenue into which came first eight lines of Metropolitan
Police, every horse in each line being a perfect match, and then
the vivid red splash of a detachment of the Royal Canadian
Mounted Police; a proud moment in an occasion that was not
only in itself historic, but which was to prove, before so many
years had passed, to have been a celebration of past history.

On 25 July 1935, 8,000 policemen of all ranks paraded in
Hyde Park before the King and Queen. This impressive ceremony was the last of the Silver Jubilee reviews, and the first time
that a reigning monarch had inspected the British police forces.
The mounted sections added a smart and colourful touch to the
march past, leading the parade with Lord Trenchard at their
head, followed by Lt-Colonel Sir Percy Laurie riding Quicksilver,
the horse wearing its war decorations. A portrait of this ceremony
was presented to Sir Percy Laurie on his and Quicksilver's retirement in July 1936.

Although the early and middle thirties were years of world
slump and of national economic and political crises, by the time
of the Silver Jubilee celebrations the financial position of the
country had improved and, to many, better times seemed only
round the corner—this despite the rise to power of Hitler and
Mussolini. Only a year later the police horses were on duty
amongst the vast, silent throngs which flocked to London to
attend the King's funeral procession. An unprecedented mass
of people, amongst which an onlooker noted the police horses,
hemmed in on all sides, yet immobile save for a flick of the tail,
a toss of the head. *Le roi est mort, vive le roi!* That same year
saw the abdication of Edward VIII and the accession of his
brother as George VI, surely the most conscientious monarch of
all time.

When war broke out in 1939 no-one could forsee how it would
begin, but bombing seemed imminent. If this happened, horses
in central London could be an added danger, and those of the
Metropolitan Police were evacuated to stables at Ascot, Alex-

andra Park and Kempton Park. They did not return to duty in London until 1941, but then remained faithfully carrying out their work, despite bombing, fire, doodle-bugs and V-2s. Like the Glasgow and other mounted sections in the country, the men were equipped with steel helmets and gas masks, but no provision could be made for the horses—and fortunately neither they nor anyone else had to contend with a gas attack.

During the war years correct training and mutual confidence between horse and rider once more won the day. Far from being a public danger on their return to war-torn London, the horses materially assisted the foot police, and three of them, Regal, Upstart and Olga, were decorated with the Dickens Medal of the People's Dispensary for Sick Animals. The presentation took place in one of the London parks, and in each case the award was made 'For Outstanding Courage during the Battle of London, while serving with the Metropolitan Police Force'. On VE Day the horses were there to protect Winston Churchill from the cheering crowds, as he made his famous V for Victory sign from a car outside the Houses of Parliament. Since those war years the police horses of London have had their full share in memorable occasions. Royal weddings; the funeral of George VI; the coronation of his daughter, Queen Elizabeth II; State visits; pageants and processions.

Looking back down the years to the history of a force like the mounted police, inevitably it is the exciting and spectacular events that stand out. It might almost appear to some that the horses of the Metropolitan Police are used mainly for charging unruly mobs and taking part in ceremonial parades, but of course nothing could be further from the truth. The mounted sections are always there to call on in times of emergency, but the lives of the vast majority of both men and horses are spent on everyday duties of patrol, as occasional escorts at public and State processions, and—primarily—as deterrents to crime.

For establishing good relations with the public, the police horse is a winner every time. Literally thousands of people are familiar with the names of Winston and Imperial, the two most famous police horses to date to have carried the Queen at the Trooping the Colour ceremony. At the headquarters of the City Police where the mounted section have their stables, a notice has had to be displayed denying admittance to the horses after 9 pm. As the sergeant says, 'The horses can't get their proper sleep otherwise!' The chief inspector of a northern branch has commented with amusement on how often he and his men are asked 'Can I give your horse a sweet?' The request is never refused, but as the inspector ruefully points out, 'It's very seldom that the donor follows up with the suggestion "Would *you* like a sweet too?"' As for Imperial, he has an enormous following of fans. Most of them offer him refreshment on sight, with the result that he is not above investigating a lady's shopping bag for himself, if his rider's attention is otherwise engaged.

Today there are about 200 trained horses on duty in the metropolitan area alone; good-looking animals that vary in character as much as humans, yet are impervious to the racket and stench of modern traffic, and many of which will, with almost equal good manners, control a football crowd, escort the winner of the Derby or provide a mount for the Queen. More than 200 years since the first two 'Persuit' horses were attached to Bow Street, well-groomed police horses with their smart riders are still an integral, and useful part of the London scene. The secret of their survival and success lies in the training they receive at the Metropolitan Police Mounted Branch Training Establishment, at **Imber Court.**

CHAPTER TWO

THE MAKING OF A POLICE HORSE

COLONEL LAURIE founded Imber Court, East Molesey, and originated the training establishment for the mounted police there in 1920. The big house, surrounded by many acres of open fields and pastures soon provided better facilities for training and recreation than any then owned by the mass of the police force. As already mentioned this was the time when, in some quarters, horses seemed doomed to fade out in favour of motor vehicles. Yet today Imber Court not only provides training for the men and horses of both the Metropolitan and the City of London police, but also caters for a number of officers from provincial mounted forces. A cosmopolitan flavour is provided by police officers from overseas, from South Africa, Nigeria, Malta, Basutoland (now Lesotho) and many other countries who come to attend the courses.

A small mystery surrounds the inclusion of a policeman from Saudi Arabia in the list of those who have been to Imber Court. The Saudi-Arabian Embassy are insistent that their country does not, in fact, possess a force of mounted police—and certainly there appears to be no record of any in Jeddah.

As for myself, a study of this international list has provided the clue to something that has puzzled me ever since a memorable visit to Jordan a few years ago. I now know why, watching the sergeant in charge of a small mounted patrol of the Jerusalem police, grooming his mare in the sandy compound of the Inn of the Good Samaritan on the road to Jericho, wafted me in thought straight back to an ex-cavalry groom of my acquaintance. The whole Jordan set-up was reminiscent of a locale in the original film of *Beau Geste*. The police post resembles a small fort, the stone stalls where the four patrol horses are tethered by head-chains could well have been there when, if ever, the Good Samaritan passed upon his way. In a fold in the parched brown-and-cement-coloured hillside behind was a glimpse of the low-slung, black hair tents of the Bedouin. The sergeant spoke no English, his mare thought little of a European stranger, but her rider wielded his grooming kit, dandy brush and body brush, with a forceful cleaning sweep on to the curry comb, in an unmistakably British manner. Even the dust-dispelling hissing from between his teeth was English-bred. Jordan has had police officers at Imber Court, and obviously the gospel is well spread.

The majority of the young remount horses that arrive at the centre for training, are unbroken three- or four-year-olds. While there is no such thing as a special breed of horse used for police work in Britain, a type half or three-quarter bred, on the lines of a medium or heavyweight hunter, is preferred. The animal must have sufficient quality to enhance the force's well-earned reputation for smartness, be not less than 15.2 hands high, and be sturdy enough to carry a minimum of twelve stone, plus equipment, for several hours at a time. Two essential qualifications are a kind, ultimately calm temperament, and good feet that will stand up to the large amount of road work demanded of a police horse.

Before 1919 the Metropolitan Police rode heavy, rather common-type horses, more on the lines of a vanner. When Colonel Laurie began his reorganisation of the force, he at once supervised the buying of the horses and gradually substituted a much finer, better-bred stamp of animal. The Colonel always bought his police horses in Yorkshire, and this practice has largely continued. The assistant commissioner 'A' Department and the chief superintendent go north twice a year, to select about ten suitable animals from those collected by agents and dealers. Appropriate horses are sometimes bought from other sources, and some are presented as gifts.

This last fact accounts for the unmistakably Arabian features, the typical 'dish' face and large eyes, of a mare I saw surveying the world from her box at Imber Court, and it seems astonishing

Mounted police carried out traffic control in Paris until 1937

Even in 1920 the Paris police horses had plenty to contend with

Warrior, an ex-charger of the first world war who became the pride of the Southampton Mounted Police

Some of the old Australian Trooper Police who helped to open up the 'out back'—1880

that quite a few ex-racehorses, given to the force, should take kindly to work on the beat after the galloping and jumping of their former life. Indeed, for animals with slightly damaged tendons, the very steadiness of police work makes it suitable. That a blood horse, brought up on the over-excitements of the race-course, will calm sufficiently to become a Metropolitan remount, speaks well for the training methods used. Lincoln Prince was a racehorse who broke down but is now perfectly sound, doing steady work. Generous Star, after winning many thousands of pounds in prize money, suddenly lost all interest in racing, but is making an excellent job of his new career. One of the best-looking horses is Bachelor Gay, a brown gelding who won his class at Dublin before being presented to the Metropolitan Police.

When the remounts first arrive at Imber Court they are housed in a special stable that contains both loose-boxes and stalls. The stalls are roomy, with kicking mats fastened to the side partitions, but the horse obviously has to be tied up. His tether rope is attached to a log with a weight at the end, which slides up and down inside a cover of piping as the animal moves his head. Few of the remounts will have ever been in a stall, and since the whole emphasis of the training at Imber Court is to take things slowly and never intentionally frighten a horse, the youngsters are kept in a box until they have settled down. They are then gradually accustomed to standing in a stall during the daytime, until eventually the vast majority will lie down and go to sleep tied up, as happily as if they were free in a loosebox. However, since all horses are individuals, there is always the odd one who regards his sliding tether rope with as much suspicion as if it were a snake, and who would no more dream of lying down in his stall than of sprouting wings like Pegasus and taking to the sky. On the other hand there is also the trusting character who, like a horse once owned by a chief inspector, will stand immovable for hours, firmly 'tied' by the end of his tether rope lying, unknotted, through a tying ring!

These young remount horses are all in the charge of permanent training staff, experienced men who normally take charge of two horses each, and who do not wear uniform whilst training. They are responsible, with the aid of an established training programme, for turning an unschooled, usually unbroken horse that starts and shies at the mere thought of his own shadow into an obedient, reliable police horse, sufficiently advanced in education to be safe around London or any city streets.

The average horse takes six or seven months to attain this goal. Since horses are, however, creatures of flesh and blood with differences in temperament, conformation and breeding, no animal is hurried beyond his capacity for learning, and the training period, as well as the training programme, is made flexible to suit individual needs.

The men who take on this task must have great patience and firmness, as well as being temperamentally suited to the particular horses they are handling. Never must they become out of temper, and an excitable trainer merely excites the horse, making him literally incapable of understanding what is required. The whole system at Imber Court is geared to avoid frightening the horses, to keeping them quiet and relaxed and therefore responsive to instruction, and is based almost entirely on a method of reward. As with the average male, the best way to a horse's affections is through his stomach, and a bowl of oats or a carrot can not only quickly take the terror out of the most alarming object, but can condition a horse's mind to obedience and to the acceptance of almost any situation. From the first day that a remount is led around Imber Court on a cavesson by his trainer, gaining confidence and becoming accustomed to all the strange sights and sounds, he is rewarded each time he does as required; if the horse does not respond, no tit-bit is forthcoming. Only a maximum of five per cent of all the horses passing through the centre fail to make the grade.

For the first six weeks the horse is schooled with the trainer working from the ground. Driving on long reins begins, straight ahead and on a circle, while the pupil learns to obey the voice, and his body is suppled, his muscles strengthened by the exercise. He is taught to move freely round the trainer and has a first introduction to 'nuisance' training, in the form of a furled flag or silent rattle, with the oat bowl always well in evidence. The

first weight felt by a young horse on his back is a driving pad—
usually unresented until the girth is tightened—followed by a
'dumb jockey'. These little contraptions with crossed 'arms' are
considered out of date by many modern horsemen, and the
mounted police have them specially made in London. Whether
the method is old-fashioned or not, it works admirably. One
accepted theory is that actual weight has small effect upon a
young horse—it is what he can see moving above and behind his
head that frightens him. The side-reins attached to cavesson and
'jockey' waggle the dummy's 'arms' as the animal moves around,
apparently giving the general effect of a rider—at any rate to
the horse!

The remount staff are adepts at long-reining, and it is
fascinating to watch an expert putting a horse through his paces.
Free-moving, well-balanced and obedient to the voice as well as
to the reins, the pupil's exhibition of change of pace and rein, of
stepping four forwards, four back, of shoulder-in and a serpentine
half-pass to left and right is a joy to watch. No novice horse
would be capable of such a polished performance, but after some
weeks of long-rein driving even a raw remount has learned a great
deal, and not many put up a real rough house when it comes to
the big moment of first being backed. Of course some are easier
than others, a few manage to dislodge their trainers, and there is
the occasional 'difficult' one, like the thoroughbred mare who
was so put out by the feel of a rider's legs to either side that she
became temporarily a nervous wreck, unwilling even to eat for
some days.

To the uninitiated the roads around the centre seem to be full
of good-looking horses ridden by expert civilians. In fact these are
the remounts undergoing traffic training, and this most necessary
exercise is one of the reasons for the permanent staff wearing
mufti. The majority of motorists will take some care when passing a 'civilian' horse, but to the unthinking any horse carrying a
uniformed policeman is automatically traffic-proof. These novices
do need consideration and room to manœuvre, because if the
traffic conditions permit they are allowed to make wide detours
round parked cars or objects they mistrust. Experience has proved

that if a young horse is neither forced nor punished, he will gradually come to accept most things, however alarming they may at
first appear.

Some of the original acreage at Imber Court has been taken
over by No. 1 District Sports Club for use as playing fields, but
that still leaves eleven or twelve acres for the horses, and there
is a refreshing atmosphere of space and air. The police show a
typical regard for their animals, as well as good business sense,
by keeping a couple of paddocks where an unsound remount
can be turned away for a month or two, a year if necessary, and
given the chance of recovery. One young mare grew herself an
entirely new hoof and became completely sound once more, with
a probable working life of fifteen or sixteen years ahead of her.
The 'regulars' also appreciate these paddocks where they are
given an occasional break from duty when opportunity permits,
a short holiday at grass where they can rest mind and body and
graze for themselves the true salts of the earth.

A circular outside manège, with high walls to preclude dis-
tractions, is an invaluable place for schooling a young horse. And
the bigger, rectangular manège happens to have exactly the same
cinder surface as that of the car park at Wembley Stadium
where contestants for the Police Horse of the Year perform their
dressage test. Jumping may seem at first glance an unnecessary
achievement for a police horse, but strange obstacles are encountered in the course of duty, particularly on the country patrols,
and the art also provides a valuable lesson in obedience, increasing confidence between horse and rider. A good selection of
fences are set up in one paddock, and different jumps dotted
around near the sloping ramp and the flight of steps, both up
and down, which help to make these horses so versatile.

A practical demonstration of the value of this kind of training
was given in the twenties, when during a disturbance in Trafalgar
Square a mounted policeman rode up the steps of the then Grand
Hotel, and prevented the place from being rushed. A jumping
lane, where the fences can be taken free from any rider, is
invaluable for schooling—and gives at least one officer the chance
to demonstrate that his mare is as obedient as any dog. He sets

her loose and stands in the middle, and she comes to call, straight to him, jumping anything that lies between them.

Unlike the other services, the police are not given any special facilities for riding in individual competitive events. It seems a pity that British police officers are not allowed to boost public relations by having the chance of becoming famous show-jumpers for instance, like Raimonde d'Inzeo. He and his brother Piero are world-famous, and Raimonde is an officer in the Carabinieri, Italy's mounted-police force which undertakes civilian crowd control. His exploits and those of The Rock, the grey, Irish-bred jumper belonging to the Carabinieri and ridden by Piero, have been followed by millions of fans, both in the flesh and on television, for years, doing nothing but good for the image of the force to which they belong.

In Britain the Metropolitan, like many branches of the mounted police, does provide a very polished and well-schooled Musical Ride, performed by ordinary duty horses collected together from various stations for a month's training beforehand. Some of the bigger shows include a Best Trained Police Horse competition. For many years the Bristol Mounted Police have been the proud possessors of a horse who must be one of the largest as well as one of the most successful in the country—Robin, a bay gelding standing seventeen and three-quarter hands high, and the winner over seven years of thirty-three awards in thirty-four competitions. Robin was the Richmond Show's champion police horse of 1966. At this show back in the twenties a police horse gave a jumping display which included leaping a table at which were seated the Prince of Wales and the Duke of York. As for the Metropolitan Police, the word 'Ethel!' is almost a magic password amongst them. This venerable grey mare from Brixton has won almost every award up and down the country open to a police horse.

Somewhere deep in every officer's heart is the secret ambition to win the exacting test at the Horse of the Year Show at Wembley Stadium, and prove his own animal the Police Horse of the Year. Also in 1966, this honour was taken by another

Bristol horse, Radcliffe. One of the big events of the season is the Metropolitan Police Horse Show, attractively staged at Imber Court. This show has a flavour of its own, with jumping and the other usual events, and competitions for the Best Trained, Best Turned Out and Handiest horse. Ridden classes demand skill in the use of sword, lance and revolver as well as a compliant, steady mount. There are exciting, exhilarating moments when galloping horses thunder in turn across the arena, their riders wielding the heads of their couched lances at the precise moment to spear a ring or peg. During the eye-catching evolutions of the Musical Ride, teams of grey, chestnut and bay horses from off the beat waltz and make catherine wheels, contrive scissors, figures of eight and a star, weave in and out in a lady's chain and end with a grand charge and salute. All of which adds up to a complicated and highly disciplined routine, only possible to perform with duty horses without weeks of specialised schooling because of the preliminary training they have all received at Imber Court when young.

Around forty years ago an indignant gentleman wrote to *The Times* demanding to know if 'there is any soundness in a policy which allows mounted policemen to waste their time training for gymkhanas and other society functions?', adding crushingly that 'a knowledge of tent-pegging never assisted a policeman in his search for a criminal'. Had that correspondent been any kind of a horseman he would have known that such training helps materially to weld man and horse into a mutually confident team, better equipped for dealing with any eventuality.

Nowadays a police officer occasionally attends a local gymkhana, if time warrants it, a pleasant duty that furthers friendly relations with the public. This is a popular commission, particularly if the officer concerned happens to ride a horse like the young one undergoing training who 'Could jump a "Grade A" course eventually—if his heart ends up in the right place!'

Inter-police shows and classes also keep men and horses keen and interested. When time allows, some branches, like that of the West Riding Constabulary, give displays where the public have an opportunity for seeing police horses being trained. Many emulate the Manchester branch and put on mounted displays and a musical ride in aid of charity. There may be only four Salford City horses nowadays, but the section is still very much a 'going concern', the officers eager to rival the high standards achieved in competitions during the time between the two wars. Those were the peak years when Lt-Colonel Sir Percy Laurie, judging at Richmond, picked on a Salford gelding called Milton for special mention; when three Salford horses won the Championship and First Prize at the International Horse Show, and one of them, Cherry Grove, was later bought by King Edward VIII.

Returning to Imber Court, probably the best-known facet of police-horse education is that called 'nuisance training'. The horses must be impervious to noise, whether it is fire-bells clanging, bands playing, or the distracting screech from a dozen rattles spun by over-enthusiastic, over-indulged supporters at a Cup Tie. Even in England there might be the moment when they had to cope with the unexpected clatter of gunfire. They must learn, too, to take no notice of flags being waved in their faces—although not all horses can be expected to display the indifference of Blenheim, a wise and experienced old black gelding from Southwark police station. He and his rider were given the job one Easter Monday of keeping a big procession marching to one side down Whitehall, so that it would enter Trafalgar Square in an orderly manner for the subsequent meeting. Not all the marchers saw eye to eye on this point, and Blenheim's rider had to use his horse to practise a little gentle persuasion by pushing. Two objectors thought they could successfully nobble this move by wrapping a large banner round Blenheim's head and upsetting him, but they had chosen the wrong horse. His total calmness during this incident was recorded by a television camera, and an onlooker was so impressed that he took the trouble to go round to Great Scotland Yard and compliment them on their horses' training.

The horses must learn to step quietly over people lying in their path and to remain quiescent in the terrifying event of fire. A

few years ago the grandstand at Richmond Horse Show caught
fire during one of the classes. Against a background of billowing
clouds of smoke and hungry flames licking up towards the sky,
amidst the din of fire-bells, the clamour of the crowd and the
frightened neighing of innumerable horses and ponies, the horses
of the mounted police paraded round the ring, steadying the
nerves of humans and equines alike by their calm obedience.
Having to enter or stand in water must give the horses no qualms,
and they must learn to remain quietly at level crossings and
beneath railway arches, whilst express trains roar past—
although the City of London horses are showing a distinct preference for the electric, rather than the steam trains that used to puff
over their heads at Ludgate Circus.

All this imperturbability is achieved by very gradual degrees,
and by an association of ideas. From the first moment a young
horse sees a furled flag or silent rattle, he connects it with food.
He eats oats while these objects are brought nearer and moved
around, he uses a flag as a platter. Eventually a flag can be
waved actually touching his eyes and face, a rattle twirled almost
in his ears, yet he associates these odd happenings only with eating. When at length his training is sufficiently advanced to dispense with the oat bowl, the connection in his mind is still a
pleasurable one.

I watched six horses, nearing the end of their time at Imber
Court, doing collective 'nuisance training' in the covered school.
They limbered up with normal school work, at trot and canter,
circling, changing the rein, half-pass and halt, all done to the
accompaniment of bands, gunfire, and shouting, produced in a
conglomeration of noise over a loudspeaker. When the real business of the day began the uproar was indescribable. Two big
fire-bells, placed only a few yards apart on the tan covering of
the school, were clanged and jangled interminably; rattles, those
fiendish, din-producing instruments beloved of football fans, were
waved in their faces and the staccato crackling of gunfire from
the amplifier added to the clamour.

The horses could scarcely have cared less. They walked and
trotted between the hazards, or stood in the middle of it all on a

Her Majesty the Queen riding Neill, and Prince Philip mounted on Linnhe. Trooping the Colour, 1967

Metropolitan Police horses led the cortège at Sir Winston Churchill's funeral

The City of London mounted police ride grey horses

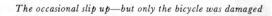

The occasional slip up—but only the bicycle was damaged

Policemen, and their horses, are there to help the public, be the methods old or new

loose rein, ears pricked, eyes calm, their minds obviously on the rewards associated with such occurrences. When the whole performance was repeated with the added complication of stepping over a 'body' on the ground they made no fuss and the dummy came to no harm. The horses may not have been quite as meticulous as they would be in avoiding stepping on real flesh and blood—which is the facet of a horse's make-up for which steeplechase jockeys are particularly thankful. More of these dummy figures are strung up in a bunch in the grounds so that the horses can be taught to push their way between, and become accustomed to the idea of people perched up above them on walls or railings.

The morning's work culminated in a posse of unmounted instructors turning themselves, with obvious relish, into a group of troublesome rowdies. Each horse in turn ignored the threatening shouts and gestures, shouldering the 'hooligans' back into a non-existent crowd with as much aplomb as though they were the dummies, attached to a trolley on wheels, with which the exercise is learned.

Obviously not every unpleasant sound can be reproduced, not every contingency catered for, and no two horses are alike, but so long as the basic training is thorough and the horse has confidence in his rider, there are few incidents with which a police horse will not cope eventually. During the last war a 'doodle-bug' exploded in the grounds of Imber Court during a sports meeting. There were several casualties amongst the visiting Welsh Guards, a police sergeant lost an eye and one horse was killed. Fortunately two of the horses there at the time were 'old stagers', back at the centre on a refresher course, and they remained completely unmoved by the whole incident, effectively calming the young horses by their example. In fact one of them, a mare, was discovered gazing interestedly over her stable door at the piles of shattered glass and rubble, her expression clearly indicating that she had decided that this was a new form of nuisance training.

Something that can never be simulated by any form of training is the atmosphere generated by a large crowd. Whether it is a demonstration where tempers run high, or whether it is a moment of national rejoicing; whether it is produced by thousands of people gathered to watch a State procession, or by the excited onlookers at a big sporting event, the emotion created at these times forms an almost tangible barrier. The horse that a police officer takes to Epsom to be ridden proudly at the head of the runners for the Derby parade down the course has to contend with this very real contingency in its strongest form. Obviously the horse, and rider, for such a job are chosen with great care; but any likely young horse has to make his debut at this type of work some time or another—and that is the moment when it is not only the horse who feels he has to 'go through it'.

For Trooping the Colour on the Queen's Official Birthday, the Queen rides a police horse. While the final choice of mount is made by Her Majesty herself shortly before the ceremony, she selects from the two or three that the police consider most suitable for the occasion. One essential qualification looked for in these horses, by both the police and Mrs Archer Houblon, who schools them beforehand, is a complete willingness to go out in front alone. This horse, above all others, will have to contend with a pent-up wall of emotion and cheering, the worst moment of all being as the Queen leaves the comparative peace of the inner quadrangle at Buckingham Palace, and rides out ahead of her escort under the centre archway.

If a remount at Imber Court is considered unready for duty after the normal training period is completed, he is kept there longer. The great majority are now taken over by their future riders. Only experienced officers are given remounts; novice riders and horses are never paired together, and care is taken to ensure that horse and rider are temperamentally suited to each other. They spend some time working together at the Centre before going on duty, so that they can come to an understanding and start creating the mutual trust that grows between a man and his horse. In Britain most officers keep to the same animal for the duration of his working life, and because of the steadiness of the work and the good care that every police horse receives, this is often at least fifteen or sixteen years. Small wonder that each officer in the mounted branches of the British police privately considers his own horse the best in the entire force !

There are other horses at Imber Court besides the remounts. All sergeants and constables belonging to the mounted section of the Metropolitan Police have to return yearly to take a refresher course, until they have completed twenty-five years' service; and the horses return for refreshers as well. Occasionally, like the big chestnut who came back in a very awkward frame of mind, determined to do the opposite to anything he was asked, these courses are essential. More often they just keep men and horses up to date, and prove a welcome break for both from the routine course of duty.

In 1839 Sir Richard Maine said that the primary object of the police is the prevention of crime. That maxim is of course as true today as it was then, and when the incidence of crime and indecency began to rise sharply in the countryside around Imber Court, it was decided to operate patrols of experienced men and trained horses from the centre. This is a fairly recent innovation and one that has met with marked success. Six horses are kept, and most of them come from ordinary street patrol, from stations like Hammersmith or Rochester Row, but sometimes a backward remount completes its training on this work. The patrols with schooled horses ride singly. They work three-hour stints, riding out six miles in all directions and usually covering about fifteen miles in all. The patrols go on through the hours of daylight, and have certainly brought a feeling of greater security to the inhabitants of the area.

As every horseman knows, a good horse deserves a good rider —and an unsupervised, inexperienced rider can spoil the best-schooled horse in a very short time, while a novice with a novice horse quickly comes to grief. So the constables who apply for transfer to the Mounted Branch of the Metropolitan Police, and who are eventually selected, are themselves trained in riding and in every aspect of horsemanship at Imber Court. Up to 1939 the majority of the applicants for the Mounted Branch were ex-cavalry men. Nowadays it is the exception, rather than the rule, to find a probationer who has ever been on the back of a horse before, let alone being a horseman. Yet despite an exacting six-month training course it is practically unknown for a man to resign, or ask to be transferred from Imber Court. No constable can become a mounted probationer until he has completed his initial two years' probation 'on the beat'; each man is put through a long and stringent process of selection before being accepted.

A few of the applicants may know a little of horses, many more may think of them as attractive animals in the abstract, but it is a fact that by the time the probationers have been taught how to look after their mounts and have learned some riding, they would not change the job for any other. In addition to the interesting work asked of the mounted police in the course of their duty, there is no doubt that the strange bond that grows between horses and those who have experience of them is a big factor in keeping this section permanently up to strength. Also, of course, there is a certain glamour attached to the force: the mounted police are renowned for their smart turnout and the appeal they make to the public.

The horses that have the important job of teaching the probationers at Imber Court live in separate stabling blocks to those inhabited by the remount and patrol horses. Each animal is cared for, groomed, fed and mucked out by the probationer who rides him, under the experienced and eagle-eyed supervision of the probationers' equitation instructors.

For the purpose of instructing, the police use horses that for one reason or another are unsuited to ordinary duty, but which make an admirable job of this one. Horses like Emma, an ex-duty mare from the stations at Southwark and Wandsworth. She is twenty years old and now not quite up to street patrol, but working on the soft tan covering of the indoor school at Imber Court suits her admirably. She is beautifully schooled and possesses a verve and enjoyment for the work that belie her age. When I watched a class of probationers practising for a test after four and a half months of training, one man was riding a big dappled grey who is no longer traffic-proof after an accident with a lorry, and who carries a scar on his flank to endorse his dislike. As with all these 'schoolmaster' horses this one looked thoroughly happy in his work—and is also obviously an animal of character with a sense of humour : each time that the class returned from canter to trot, preparatory to going off on the other leg on a figure of eight, the grey signified his disapproval of his rider's aids—with a squeal and a buck just big enough to shoot the discomfited young man's cap over his nose.

At the end of their six-month training course the Metropolitan probationers are posted to one of the twenty-four police stables in the metropolitan area as mounted reserves, but even then they do not immediately receive a horse of their own. As a reserve a man remains on probation, riding the horses of officers absent from duty, until the day comes when he is appointed to mounted duty on an allocated horse. Then, for the first time, he can regard himself as a fully fledged member of the Mounted Branch, and look forward to years of comradeship with an animal that is, to all intents and purposes, his own.

CHAPTER THREE

NO DUTY COMES AMISS

THE fifth Earl of Lonsdale was born in 1857. During the eighty-seven years of his long life he was renowned as a champion of all forms of sport, including anything connected with horses. Even at the dramatic moment when huge crowds assembled outside Buckingham Palace on a sultry August evening in 1914 to cheer the Royal Family with patriotic fervour on the declaration of war, the well-known sporting figure of the Earl was to be seen in company with an equine : to be exact, with the donkey belonging to one of his coster protégés in whose company he was watching the spectacle.

At different times Lord Lonsdale was Master of Foxhounds of both the Woodland Pytchley and the Quorn hunts, and in 1907 he became president of the first International Horse Show, held at Olympia. He was a first-class whip and a great patron of the road. On the occasion of the marriage of George V, then Duke of York, to Princess Mary of Teck, Lord Lonsdale presented the royal couple with a large carriage with a folding hood, a novelty which the Earl claimed to have invented. The vehicle became known as a Lonsdale waggonette, despite Sir Walter Gilbey's caustic observation that amongst three other claimants to the invention was a certain Mr Robertson, who said he had built a carriage with just such a hood twenty-nine years previously. Anyway the Lonsdale waggonette was in frequent use at Balmoral, and is now in the Royal Mews at Buckingham Palace.

It was an American-type buggy that Lord Lonsdale used in carrying out his great driving feat of 1891, when 'he undertook to drive four stages of five miles within an hour, using for the first three stages one (horse), a pair, a team, and riding postilion in the fourth'. But whatever kind of carriages the sporting Earl used when in London, he housed them together with the horses, in an elegant coach-house and stabling built for him just off Whitehall. It was in keeping with his deep interest in horses that in 1925 the Earl made over this building to the Mounted Section of the Metropolitan Police. Great Scotland Yard has remained the headquarters of No. 1 District, Mounted Branch, ever since.

Except for the removal of the glass-fronted doors through which his Lordship's handsome vehicles could be admired, and for a re-arrangement of the administrative offices, Great Scotland Yard today is exactly as it was when the police took it over. The fourteen horses now housed there come in off duty on the street under the same archway that used to echo with the rumble and clatter of a carriage and pair. They still go upstairs to bed, stamping up a gentle winding slope carpeted with coconut matting, to the stalls and loose-boxes used by their predecessors. Since the majority of the Metropolitan horses are bred in Yorkshire, there may be even a blood tie between them and those carriage horses of long ago. For Yorkshire is the home of that most versatile and all-round animal, the Cleveland Bay. Today this horse, whose ancestors were the sturdy chapmen's horses that walked the Yorkshire Dales carrying a pedlar's pack, is frequently used in cross-breeding to produce the useful type of weight-carrying hunter preferred by the mounted police. In Lord Lonsdale's day a slightly different stamp of the breed, longer in the leg and with a more showy action produced through an infusion of thoroughbred blood, was much sought after to draw the carriages of the élite. Cleveland Bays are used as carriage horses in the Royal Mews today.

Unlike the New York Police who have civilian grooms, until they reach the rank of inspector the officers of the Metropolitan Police look after their own horses, just as they did as probationers at Imber Court. They work an eight-hour day, coming on duty at different times to fit in with the various street patrols, and each horse is ridden daily for three hours on this duty, with one day of rest a week. On special occasions both horse and rider may be on duty for anything up to ten hours.

All police stables are run to a routine and since the majority of the Metropolitan horses are more or less of a type and size, a standard feeding ration is feasible. Nevertheless the ration can if necessary be varied to suit individual tastes, as can the bedding : each horse is issued with ten pounds of wheat straw per day, but there is occasionally a good reason for substituting peat. For instance, Harmony, a bay gelding, an elderly resident of King's Cross police station, had a passion for eating his bed. A reliable old horse of the type known as a 'senior officer's ride', he occasioned much concern when he was discovered cast in his stall one morning. The cause was traced to rolling during an attack of colic, brought on, it was thought, by his greedy habit. At any rate a change was made in his bedding, and Harmony, his eating confined to his meal times, returned to duty on the beat.

Unlike army chargers, who all wear the standard army saddle, fitted by the use of a folded blanket underneath, every Metropolitan and City police horse is issued with his own individual saddle-tree. Whatever-sized saddle is put on top of this, the tree and the girth that goes with it remain with the horse for his whole working life.

Unlike the majority of police in other countries, the British police are unarmed, and the two apparent 'holsters' (wallets, to give them their official name) on each side of a Metropolitan saddle contain nothing more lethal than a short truncheon, a linen nose-bag, a waterproof saddle cover and a first-aid kit. From personal experience I can vouch for the fact that these wallets, pressing against the knees, can be invaluable for keeping a moderate rider 'in the plate' on a bucking horse, when stirrups and reins have already gone for six !

The Metropolitan and City Mounted Police and many of the provincial branches carry a long baton-truncheon, officially a mounted patent truncheon, with a sword handle, and similar to those used by the Norwegian and Dutch mounted police. In England it is many years since these weapons have been drawn in anger, but when they were first introduced some time in the twenties a newspaper correspondent observed that 'a substitution of a long stick for the truncheon has proved of great value, and since its introduction there has been no casualty to either horse or men on duty with crowds'. An ambiguous reflection that seems to call for the services of a cartoonist.

The horses wear breastplates which look well and prevent the saddle from slipping back, and in Britain most police horses, including all those of the Metropolitan Branch, wear a collar chain. This device, not unlike a chain martingale, normally hooks on to a 'D' in front of the saddle bow, with the other end snapped to the head-collar. During those years between the two world wars when demonstrations tended to get rough, it occurred to some of the rowdies that if they cut a mounted policeman's reins he would be left in the position of a rudderless boat, but collar chains put paid to that bright idea. If an officer anticipates trouble he has only to attach the chains to the bit to have a pair of reins that will defy any cutting.

Both Dutch and German police horses wear dropped nose-bands and snaffle bits, but with the exception of the remounts, whose first bit is a snaffle, British police horses wear the well-proved army 'universal pelham'—with a higher 'port' in the centre for use with those few tiresome animals who persist in putting their tongues over the top.

On special occasions horses ridden by senior officers of the mounted branches wear ceremonial bridles, often ornamented with decorations like the red and blue 'beards' usually sported by the animal ridden by London's City Marshal, the bits adorned with the long, curved cheekpieces of days gone by. For the Trooping the Colour the horse carrying the Queen wears a double bridle to which, together with a side-saddle, he is re-accustomed each year by Mrs. Archer Houblon. All the horses supplied by the Metropolitan Police on this occasion, for use by members of the Royal Family and Household and senior army officers, wear red or blue silk rosettes adorning the ceremonial bridles, which mostly come from the Royal Mews.

In 1937 the police horse Cobham was bought as King George VI's personal charger, and ever since 1948 a horse belonging to the Metropolitan Police has carried the Queen at her Official Birthday Parade. Trooping the Colour is consequently the most important ceremony of the year for the force. The first time the Queen, then Princess Elizabeth, attended the parade on horseback, she was mounted on an ex-hunter, Tommy, and was accompanying her father the King; by the next year the King was not well enough to ride, and the Princess rode the police horse Winston beside her father's carriage. She continued to ride this horse, up to and after her accession in 1952, until Winston's death as the result of a street accident, five years later. Winston, a big fine-looking chestnut, was stabled at Great Scotland Yard, and his successor Imperial, another handsome chestnut, is also stabled there. So too is Doctor, the grey horse of admirable disposition who carried the Queen in 1963 when Imperial was lame, and again in 1966. The big seventeen-hand bay mare, Linnhe, used several times by Prince Philip for the Trooping, has been supplied by the Cannon Row police stables.

Mounted police the world over take part in a great many ceremonial occasions, and however meticulous the organisation there must still be the occasional moment of drama, as well as those untoward or hilarious incidents which the organising officials pray hard will never occur.

During the brief months of Edward VIII's reign, the King presented new colours to six battalions of the Guards at a brilliant military ceremony in Hyde Park on 16 July 1936. As the King rode back past the cheering crowds to Buckingham Palace, there was a sudden disturbance as he reached the top of Constitution Hill, and a man hurled a revolver into the roadway. The King rode imperturbably upon his way, and foot police arrested the offender with the aid of a mounted policeman.

When European royalty were on a State visit to Holland, a detachment of the Dutch Mounted State Police were stationed behind an army trooper responsible for hauling up the Royal Standard of the country concerned at the appropriate moment. Bands played, the royal barge approached, the trooper set about his particular duty—one good pull and the halyard snapped! A conveniently placed tub of flowers made soft landing for the trooper's involuntary sit-down, and years of discipline just coped with the Dutch mounted policemens' robust sense of humour.

That Dutch trooper's discomfiture can have been no worse than that of the Commissioner of the Metropolitan Police on one day many years ago. The King and Queen were returning from a visit abroad and a State drive had been arranged from Waterloo station to Buckingham Palace. As the crowds began to assemble and the time for their majesties' arrival drew near, the Commissioner, decked out in all his ceremonial glory, rode up to take position in front of the archway of the Members' Entrance to the County Hall.

No one will ever know what got into that normally most mannered of all police horses on that day. Maybe a horse-fly was probing beneath the ornamental saddle-cloth, maybe he was just plain bored. Whatever the cause, the animal began to up-end his hinder half, at first with moderation, then, as the crowd began to take notice and enjoy the situation, with increasing violence. 'Ride 'im cowboy!' yelled the inevitable wit, and to a roar of laughter the Commissioner, by now acutely conscious that a ceremonial uniform is no gear in which to ride a bucking horse, thankfully sought refuge in the exercising possibilities of the County Hall car park. He re-appeared on time, his mount once more properly sober and gentlemanly.

All the ceremonial saddlery from the Royal Mews worn by the Metropolitan Police horses at the Trooping the Colour is beautiful but extremely old, and occasionally a strap or buckle snaps at a crucial moment. A senior member of the Royal Household once discovered to his horror that one side of the ornamental bit was hanging useless from his horse's mouth. Fortunately, being a police horse and well-versed in the requirements of the ceremony, the animal proceeded calmly on his way down the Mall. On the wide open spaces of Horseguards Parade he responded to leg aids, combined with the efforts of the officer's immediate companions, who veered in on each side to steer horse and rider into position.

Each day there are Guardsmen to be escorted to and from Buckingham Palace for the Changing of the Guard; and police horses accompany the King's Troop when they clatter off to Hyde Park to fire salutes for royal birthdays and State visits. On a

day of brilliant sunshine in May 1967, a contingent of Metropolitan mounted policemen provided part of the escort when the
Queen and King Faisal of Saudi Arabia drove in procession to
Hyde Park to review the King's Troop: this inspection was
taking place for the first time since 1873, when Queen Victoria,
in honour of the Shah of Persia, with him reviewed a parade of
the Troop on Smith's Lawn at Windsor.

Royal visits are looked on more as ceremonial events than as
venues for political negotiations, but King Faisal arrived in England at a crucial moment in the normally critical affairs of the
Middle East. This was the first time that any ruler of Saudi Arabia
had come to this country in an official capacity, and it took place
at a moment when Britain was in the process of pulling out of
the Arabian and Gulf areas, and when the problem of with-
drawal from Aden was at boiling point. Suddenly a country that
was founded by King Faisal's father, Abdul Aziz ibn Saud, only
sixty or so years ago, when he took the capital of Riyadh single
handed and finally spread his rule from the Persian Gulf to the
Red Sea, was stepping into the modern world, perhaps to take
over Middle Eastern responsibilities being laid down by Britain.

On that May morning, only forty years since the Ikhwan, the
Brethren, were still galloping over the Jordan border from Saudi
Arabia, raiding, and bringing by the sword their fanatical inter-
pretation of a purer Muslim religion, King Faisal sat beside the
British Queen, as the King's Troop in ceremonial cuirass and
plumed busby, jingled by on horseback at the walk, wheeled
and came back at the gallop, hooves thundering, gun-carriages
swaying. A magnificent horseman himself, this hawk-faced Arabian King would particularly appreciate the return, still at the
gallop, when one from each of the leading six couples of riders
leaped from his horse in front of the Queen, while his mount
was led off still at the canter. Almost in the same moment the
guns came back full tilt, the gun-carriages were galloped away
and the cannon roared, first singly and then altogether—an ear-
splitting royal salute, not entirely appreciated by one police horse
on crowd patrol.

Always when foreign royalty come to England and drive in

state through the London streets, the police escort, as on this occasion, consists of nine grey horses—led by a chief inspector out in front of four mounted officers, with the other four bringing up the rear of the procession. A brave sight, if dwarfed by the Dutch Queen's forty-eight mounted policemen, twenty-four in front and twenty-four behind, who provide an escort for her State drives through the streets of The Hague.

Police horses have their role to play at the annual State opening of Parliament, at royal or 'society' weddings, and at weddings of stage, screen and television personalities. A coronation, like the magnificent ceremony when Queen Elizabeth II drove in the great golden State Coach, drawn by six Windsor Greys, from the Palace to her crowning at Westminster Abbey, draws vast crowds and calls for months of preparation by the police, both foot and mounted.

One energetic and relatively onerous duty for the two police officers and horses involved is that of providing an escort when a new Ambassador drives to Buckingham Palace to present his credentials to the Queen. However heavy the traffic no further police escort is provided, and it requires good judgment and organisation to ensure that the three carriages that normally make up the entourage arrive at the Palace at five minutes to mid-day. The Queen receives Ambassadors at noon exactly, and this is one appointment for which it is considered unthinkable to be late.

The two police officers ride first to the Royal Mews to pick up the carriages. One of these may be the maroon-coloured Town Coach known as King Edward VII's that was kept at Windsor for many years before being brought back to the Royal Mews in London. Renovated in 1963, it is the only one of its type remaining in the Mews; several were disposed of during world war II. The other carriages frequently used for conveying an Ambassador and his Embassy staff to Buckingham Palace are State landaus. A number of these vehicles, purchased for Queen Victoria between 1838 and 1872, are still in use. Both types of carriage are normally drawn by a pair of horses, frequently Cleveland Bays, driven from the box.

The cavalcade sets off with one police officer riding in front to watch the flux of traffic, and the other riding behind the last carriage to stop any overtaking. The first port of call is St James' Palace for the Marshal of the Diplomatic Corps, and then on to the Embassy concerned or to the Ambassador's private residence. The entire operation is timed to be taken at a moderate trot, but events can be disruptive; despite every effort by the leading police officer a snarl-up in the traffic can lose precious minutes. Those are the occasions when the remainder of the journey to the Palace has to be taken at a spanking rather than a moderate trot, and also underline the necessity for both police and carriage horses to be fit. A sweating horse is no credit to either rider or coachman, and since there is usually a wait of twenty minutes or so at the Palace, it would be unsightly, and certainly unwise from a health point of view, for the animals to stand in a cloud of their own steam.

The return journey is taken at the same pace. There may be a further wait at the Embassy, while the Diplomatic Marshal is offered refreshment before being taken back to St James' Palace; and the day's duty as Ambassador's escort can involve long hours and perhaps a sixteen-mile trot in all.

Police horses are on duty each year on that day in spring when boisterous crowds, sporting dark or light blue favours, throng Putney Bridge and the river banks to cheer on the University boat race; the horses also attend rugger matches at Twickenham. Every November they stand at the Cenotaph.

As well as having unchallenged usefulness in crowds, the mounted sections can take the same responsibilities as the foot police when it comes to regulating traffic, crime or any contingency requiring police intervention. If a mounted policeman on street patrol comes upon a traffic block, however caused, he does his best to sort out the tangle—and has the advantage over his pedestrian colleague in being higher above the vehicles. The horse's thorough training comes to the fore as he stands motionless on a loose rein, surrounded by buses and motor bicycles, lorries and taxicabs, while his rider uses one or both arms to direct operations.

Just how the horses of today, no less sensitive and highly strung than their forebears, do become inured to the racket and stench and terrifying proximity of the glut of town and city traffic is little short of miraculous. Even amongst police horses some are more traffic-proof than others, of course, just as some vehicles prove more frightening. An officer of the City mounted police has vivid cause for remembering the days when the breweries still used steam wagons for transporting their wares. One of these monsters, puffing smoke and steam, the glow from its firebox adding to its fearsome appearance, came trundling up behind him as he rode on street patrol around the City. This apparition was more than his horse was prepared to stomach, and to the driver's surprise and the officer's embarrassment, that load of beer barrels was provided with an involuntary lead escort for a mile or so down the road.

On the other hand there are horses like a brown gelding stabled at Great Scotland Yard. King, an ex-racehorse, owning The Tetrach amongst his more illustrious ancestors, is impervious to traffic, but dislikes cheering crowds and brass bands. Brig o' Dee, that handsome horse presented to the mounted police by the Queen Mother because jumping was not to his taste, has gone down in history for showing an equal aversion for the trappings of ceremonial. An excellent horse on street patrol, Brig o' Dee once scattered his rider's decorations along the Mall as he returned hurriedly from the dress rehearsal of the Trooping the Colour, well in advance of the mounted band and sovereign's escort.

As for crime, it must have been a startled bandit who, in this motorised age, heard the clatter of horse's hooves behind him, seconds after he had snatched a money bag from a bank messenger. Away went the thief, reasonably confident of shaking off this unexpected but apparently cumbersome pursuer by dodging in and out of the traffic and passers-by. Not for nothing however are police horses schooled to be so well balanced that they can strike off into a canter from a standstill and, if the necessity arises, neckrein at speed as handily as a polo pony. Dodge where he would, the chase was quickly over and the miscreant arrested, cursing the ill-luck that sent along a police horse on street patrol at that particular moment. Another police horse on duty in the East End was instrumental in apprehending a vanload of tobacco stolen from a loading bay. The driver caught sight of the approaching officer and accelerated quickly away, but not before his number had been noted. The policeman galloped off in pursuit and had the satisfaction of catching up and arresting the driver when the van was eventually held up at traffic lights. Such incidents are exceptional, but they prove the versatility of a mounted policeman.

The total strength of the Metropolitan Mounted Police is around 210 officers and 201 horses, and these are stationed at the twenty-four stables apportioned amongst the four Divisions of the Metropolitan area. No. I District, which is responsible for the West End of London, has a complement of sixty horses. Some of the stables are large, Hammersmith taking nineteen horses, some accommodate as few as three. Some stables are old, like that at Kings Cross where the horses live in the kind of old-fashioned but comfortable stall used when *Black Beauty* was written. These seven horses sometimes have Sunday duty because they live in the Arsenal area, and come out to supervise the fans who queue up to buy Cup Final tickets, day of rest regardless.

There are Metropolitan stables in the East End where the officers keep a friendly eye on the treatment and condition of the coster ponies, others at Brixton and Southwark and Hyde Park. At outlying places like West Hampstead and Epsom, where the stabling is new, the work consists largely of country patrols, over the heaths and downs, a modern version of the duties for which Peel's mounted police were originally conceived. Highwaymen may no longer be their concern but in addition to the proved preventive effect of mounted patrols, the horses are an immense asset when it comes to searching such areas for lost children or for suspected criminals on the run. They can quickly cover a wide area in difficult going, and a horse on soft ground can come close up to a suspect before his presence is detected. Horses were used, for instance when a young man murdered his step-sister and fled north of the Thames to the windswept, watery spaces of Dagenham Marshes.

In 1966 three police officers cruising around a London suburb in a patrol car signalled to the driver of a van to stop his vehicle. Within minutes, they were lying shot in the road. The killing horrified and inflamed the whole country and sparked off one of the most intensive murder hunts of all time. Two of the killers were captured within a short while, but the third, a man named Roberts, was on the run for several months. An ex-Commando, Roberts was well versed in the art of self-preservation, and after the theft of some camping kit, part of the search was concentrated on tracts of rough countryside. When a possible hide-out was discovered in Epping Forest the mounted patrols were called in; and this was one of the occasions when they used 'walkie-talkie' sets. With the aid of the horses the forest was combed but the bird had flown. Eventually Roberts's camp was found in another part of the country and he was arrested.

Around 1962 an alarming number of women and children were being molested in a countrified area not far from London. At that time the country patrols were something of an innovation, but it was thought worth while trying out the deterrent effect of a horse patrol, an enterprise that proved entirely satisfactory. Six horses were sent to the area for the summer, and housed in the old stabling attached to a property used as a police sports centre. One member of the patrol slept there at night to keep an eye on the horses.

The house is old, built on the site of one even more ancient, and if the patrol heard rumours of the place being haunted they paid scant heed. Certainly the constable who had been there on night duty for the past six weeks was not concerned with apparitions. Not, that is, until the night when he woke suddenly at 2 am with his heart thumping and the eerie certainty that some noise outside the margin of reason had disturbed him. As he tried to collect his wits it came again, the clear and distinct sound of the scrape . . . scrape . . . of a boot and a rattling of chains. The constable confesses to being no hero and his immediate reaction was to stay put. Then he rose and peered out of the French windows that open on to a courtyard separating the house from the stables. There was nothing there. The buildings showed grey and silent in the moonlight; a huge boulder, used for centuries as a mounting block, threw its long shadow across the paving stones.

Eventually the constable returned to bed determined to dash to the window on any untoward sound, but the remainder of the night passed uneventfully. When his relief arrived at six o'clock next morning, the constable told him of the noise, adding that he reckoned 'it must have been the old ghost'. The remark gained him merely a speculative look. The weeks passed and the episode was forgotten. Then, at a gymkhana held at the sports centre, the constable overheard an elderly man, obviously on familiar ground, say to his wife, 'The mounting block's still here,' and was sufficiently curious to get into conversation. The wife, who had been lady's maid to the family living in the house many years ago, asked a question that nearly shot the constable out of his regulation boots : 'Have you ever heard the ghost?'

Apparently the house staff had quite frequently called the local police to investigate an unexplained noise of rattling chains. The husband had been one of these policemen, and he corroborated how doors in the house used to open for no reason, and how the police had found a secret tunnel to the nearby church. The story of the ghost is of some unfortunate who lived in the original house centuries ago and who dared to profess a religion different from that of his neighbours. He was born club-footed, and used to drag his deformity around the big rooms and up the tunnel to the little church. His foot precluded escape on the night his neighbours came, bound him with chains, and burned the house down around him.

On reflection, the constable thinks a coincidence of trivial happenings may explain the noise he heard. The stabling was old, the stalls with iron mangers and the horses tied with chains attached to a sliding weight, like those in the remount stable at Imber Court, the flooring of small, old-fashioned stone insets. That night, just as on those nights of years ago, a horse preparing to lie down scraped through its bedding with the tip of its shoe, as horses will, before rattling its head chain against the manger as it went down. At that moment, and in an otherwise still night, some errant puff of wind carried the sound across the courtyard before dying away in its own breath. And to a startled sleeper, in the moonlit calm of the small hours, alone in the countryside where sounds and shadows take on a weird composition of their own, the familiarity of these sounds could be lost.

Now the old stabling is lost beneath the foundations of the smart new police station housing a permanent patrol. The horses sleep untied in looseboxes, the flooring is not of stone insets; does anyone now hear the scraping of a club-foot across the floor, the rattle of a chain?

CHAPTER FOUR

AROUND BRITAIN

THERE are five horses in London who work a different type of country patrol from that once disturbed by a ghost. Strictly speaking they are not police horses at all, but since they and their riders 'police' the areas where they are kept, they deserve mention. These are the animals under the jurisdiction of the Bailiff of the Royal Parks Division, part of the Ministry of Public Buildings & Works.

The Mounted Park-Keeper force was formed in 1950. Three horses are stabled at Richmond Park and two at Bushey Park, all looked after by their riders. They are big, good-class animals with a previous history of hacking or hunting, and they carry the park keepers on their rounds amongst the trees and herds of deer, and over the green acres where they work; a pleasant life for both men and horses, especially in the spring and summer, with little road work and no fast traffic, and amongst surroundings where the value of a horse is obvious.

If you stroll up Cheapside, or anywhere in that congested square mile lying beneath the shadow of St Paul's Cathedral that is called the City, and see a policeman riding a grey horse with a red-and-white striped browband to its bridle, you will know that horse and rider belong to another force entirely separate from the Metropolitan Mounted Branch, the City of London Police.

The horse section of this force was formed in 1931, but the City Police themselves were formed in 1839, modelled, of necessity if unwillingly, on Sir Robert Peel's efficient Metropolitan Police Force created some years previously. Even before 1839 the good citizens who lived within the ancient boundaries, under the jurisdiction of the Lord Mayor and Corporation, had been forced to add a hundred day-police to the privately employed, miscellaneous collection of watchmen and beadles who guarded their property by night. However much people in theory preferred the old-time 'Charlies' to any newly organised, disciplined, state-paid constabulary, the fact was that Sir Robert Peel's Bobbies were proving so efficient that hosts of footpads, rogues and robbers were crossing the boundaries from the Metropolitan area, and taking up residence amongst the criss-crossed narrow streets and crowded warehouses of the City.

Before 1931 the City Police hired horses from various carriers as the need arose, and when the small mounted section was first formed, the horses were kept at the City Greenyard, an old-established building which could house anything from a stray cat to a cow. These stables were blitzed on a December night in 1940, and the horses were evacuated to Staffordshire for the duration.

In 1946 when the war was over and both people and institutions were picking up the threads again, the City Police decided once more to establish a horse patrol. The numbers were built up from two to six horses, and stabling was offered by the brewing firm of Whitbreads. For the next twenty years the horses had quarters within the building used by the brewery's huge Shire horses. All through those years the Mounted Branch received every possible kindness and consideration, until in 1966 the horses could be moved into new stables attached to the modern police station off Cheapside.

Here the accommodation is as up to date and comfortable as any in the country. The normal strength of the section is six horses, but if a good one turns up in the meantime, there is room for it in one of the eight looseboxes; another is set aside as a 'sick box'. Water power points are provided for washing down the floors, and an electric boiler copes with every equine requirement. As in most current accommodation storage space is inadequate and hay cannot be bought in bulk, but the adjoining tack-cleaning and saddle rooms are both handy and well-equipped, and showers—very welcome after spells of duty—are installed for the comfort of the sergeant and ten constables who make up the section.

About ten years after the war it was decided to buy only grey horses for the section—an attractive idea with only one snag attached : grey horses do moult for most of the year, and there is no better medium for showing up stray grey and white hairs than the navy blue of a policeman's uniform! Since all greys are dark as foals, there are now six or seven animals in attractive shades, varying from the iron-grey of a five-year-old to the almost pure white of the old horse that has carried the chief superintendent at the Lord Mayor's Show for some years—a good-tempered animal, whose large stature and lengthy ears have provoked students lining the route for the occasion to greet him and his rider with the chant 'M-U-F-F-I-N spells MUFFIN!' in teasing reference to Muffin the Mule, the famous children's cartoon character. In fact since 1962 whatever nicknames they may earn, the City Police horses have been given names with some City connection—such as Walbrook, Templar or Cromwell—unlike those of the Metropolitan Police, which are all christened with the same first letter in the same year.

Originally most of the City horses were of Irish extraction, bought from the same dealer in Gloucestershire who supplied Birmingham and Bristol, but nowadays they come from any source that can produce the required type and temperament. Perhaps even more than the Metropolitan Police horses, those destined to patrol the streets of the City have to be steadily well-mannered from the moment they complete their initial training at Imber Court. There are no parks or open spaces in the City, no quiet backwaters, no broad roadways like the Mall where a young horse can be gradually introduced to traffic chaos. City horses step straight out of their stable into the roaring conglomeration of buses, lorries, pantechnicons, taxicabs and vans that throttle the teeming streets lying between the Thames and Bishopsgate, Aldgate and Holborn. These horses share with those of the Metropolitan Police the privilege of exercising in the covered school at Buckingham Palace; and a good friend lends them a field at Chingford during the summer, where they can practice for the Police Show and other competitions. The branch owns a two-horse trailer which is utilised to some extent on these occasions—a good hour is needed to hack out to the field—and for such a small section it has always given an excellent account of itself at the Metropolitan Police Horse Show at Imber Court, and at other police shows round the country. The branch is justifiably proud of the keenness of its men and horses.

Keeping law and order in the City is a specialised task, different from police work in the Metropolitan area and possibly anywhere else in Britain. Each day around half a million people surge into this congested district, but once the working day is over, Christopher Wren's masterpiece, St Paul's, is left to brood . over innumerable blocks of offices and millions of square feet of warehouses, inhabited for the night only by cats, with here and there a privately employed guard or watchman. So the majority of crimes encountered by the City Police come into the category of breaking and entering, mostly under cover of darkness—offences and circumstances for which mounted patrols are not best suited. The Mounted Branch of the City Police, as of the Metropolitan, is most valued for its routine street work, for its work in crowd control and at official ceremonies.

Some of these ceremonies are connected solely with the City and Guildhall, that Town Hall of the City of London, most of which was destroyed by the Great Fire of 1666, but which was rebuilt soon after and survived the bombing of 1941. When Royalty or foreign dignitaries visit the Guildhall, or attend a banquet in the Egyptian Hall of the Mansion House—the 200-year-old official residence of the Lord Mayors of London—the police horses duly help to provide an escort or marshal the crowds, borrowing support from the mounted men at Great Scotland Yard when necessary. The Lord Mayor's Show is the year's climax in ceremonial duty, a pageant that the City claims entirely for itself. On that day the beautiful ceremonial saddle-cloth and bridle belonging to the City Marshal, brought out from their sanctum in the City stabling, have for many years been fitted on the broad back and noble head of Alamein, a wise old grey from Southwark, who has in the past carried the Duke of Edinburgh at the Trooping the Colour. On that day, too, the weighty, gilt-encrusted, centuries-old Lord Mayor's coach is man-handled out of the specially adapted coach house at Whitbread's Brewery where it lodges, and harnessed up with six magnificent Shires, Whitbread horses which some years ago replaced the lighter carriage horses. From Ewer Street, from the quiet recesses under the railway arches by Charing Cross, three more semi-State and aldermen's coaches are trundled from the half-light of years gone by, to join the numbers of floats and set pieces, all illustrating the theme of that year's pageant, which make up the procession.

These are the highlights. For the rest of the year, day in and day out, come rain come shine, the officers who ride the grey horses with browbands picked out in the colours of their district, will be on street patrol, taking in their stride all the normal duties of the foot police. There are traffic snarls to disentangle, people to direct and aid. There is occasional drama : when a man falls off scaffolding to land at the feet of a police horse; or a corporation horse falls into a manhole and has to be rescued by the fire brigade, with the special apparatus which that versatile body keep for the purpose. Always there are those two intangible jobs at which not only the City and Metropolitan but all police horses have no equal—getting on a friendly footing with the public, and providing a deterrent to crime.

The number of horses in each mounted section around the cities and towns of Britain varies considerably. In Newcastle upon Tyne, for instance, the City Police Force was formed in 1836, and was allocated three horses for use on night patrols, at an annual outlay of £78. A specified Mounted Section gradually evolved as motor vehicles superseded horses for transport, and today the City and County Constabulary of Newcastle upon Tyne have a mounted branch of six. The horses are used principally for patrolling the 970 acres of parks and woodlands around the city—an enviable job in good weather for the sergeant and five constables, who can occasionally be seen enjoying a good training gallop across the moors, as a change from the more sober paces of patrol work.

A radio telephone, used on country patrol

Imperial, one of the Queen's best known and favourite mounts for Trooping the Colour, competing at Richmond

'Nuisance Training'. Police horses must learn to accept even gunfire

There are twenty-seven police horses in Liverpool; only one, a Yorkshire-bred dark bay gelding called Kim, in Brighton. Edinburgh boasted a strength of four sergeants and forty-six constables in 1902, all mounted on hirelings and used almost exclusively on ceremonial escort. By 1931 this Mounted Branch had twelve horses of its own; the number was reduced to six, at which it has been maintained, after world war II. Kingston upon Hull began with four horses some time before 1934. During the 1939-45 war, two of them were sold and two turned out to grass, which proved to be a fortunate decision as the police stables were demolished by a bomb. The section was re-formed in 1949 with the same number of horses. Manchester has twenty horses; Bristol has actually increased their numbers from the original nine of 1897 to twelve animals proudly owned today.

The British provincial mounted sections show a catholic taste in their choice of horses' names. There is an appealing sound about Miss Bexley, a bay mare at Salford. In Hull the City Fathers take on the official christening of the police horses, choosing names with a local connection; Fairfax is called after an intrepid general who helped to close the city against the Royalists in the Civil Wars, Haworth and Maister commemorate notable houses. William Wilberforce, the Member of Parliament who devoted his life to the abolition of the slave trade, has his surname perpetuated by a police horse patrolling the streets of his birthplace. Manchester goes in for Charles Dickens characters, and surely the lucky officer who rides a horse called Snodgrass must have the handling of a distinct personality.

As with police horses the world over, most of the animals of the provincial mounted sections anywhere in Britain have a similar routine of regular work. The variations come with the different functions connected with their particular town or city, or owing to some local deviation of the countryside. The Mounted Branch of the Lancashire Constabulary carries out patrols in the Lake District during Bank Holiday periods, principally to restrain litter-louts and to protect National Trust properties from damage. These men and horses also have the thrills and responsibilities of race meetings at Haydock Park and Aintree. In recent years this duty no longer means coping only with the day of the National or other race-meetings, but includes patrolling the course beforehand, to deter vandals from damaging the fences and stands.

Sport, such as international Rugger matches, county cricket, football at Manchester, and the weekly matches of the Everton and Liverpool Football Clubs, which often attract 45,000 spectators, obviously provide work in crowd control. The mounted men are indispensable for searching terrain that is difficult for foot police and impassable to cars. In Salford, parks and open drains get particular attention from the policemen with their horses during the school holidays. And although in Britain the mounted sections seldom work at night, unlike their counterparts in New York, Iran and other countries, the Salford City police provide for the possibility by issuing stirrup lamps for late duty— an essential for any horseman in the dark.

At one time the Southampton Police had a mounted section, and the Recorder of Southampton used to be driven to court in a carriage and pair, accompained by a mounted policeman. Nowadays this particular tradition is preserved only in Bristol, where nine of the mounted men escort the Lord Mayor's Coach conveying the judges to the assize court.

In 1897 the horses of the West Riding Constabulary were kept in small units dispersed amongst the towns in the police area. Today the fifteen horses of the section are stabled at Pontefract and Harrogate, with two Land-Rovers and trailers to whisk them to any district requiring them. The three-and-a-half-hour daily patrol takes the men and horses into many miles of remote and sparsely populated countryside, which the foot police find difficult to cover, and can do much to check the dumping of rubbish and old cars, scattering of litter and wanton damage.

Edinburgh, Auld Reekie, is the capital of Scotland—and Holyrood House, one-time home of the ill-starred Mary Queen of Scots, is still a royal residence. These two facts alone provide the Mounted Branch of the City of Edinburgh Police with much escort and crowd-control duty connected with ceremonial. In addition, the fame of the annual Festival and Military Tattoo brings foreign visitors flocking to the grey stone city, and its police horses can lay claim to being some of the most-photographed animals in the mounted forces of the British Isles. Yet the work which this branch finds the most rewarding of all, and certainly that which gives most pleasure to the recipients, is to be invited to send an officer and his horse to a school for spastics or for mentally retarded children, in order to give live illustration to a talk on animals.

Some years ago the British Home Office gave permission for a mounted policeman to be employed on work that must be unique in Britain, if not the world. Beachy Head, a sheer cliff-face rearing out of the sea, is the apex of the 5,000 mostly uncultivated acres that extend from the seaside town of Eastbourne to Birling Gap. This tract of downland remains mercifully undeveloped, an unspoilt delight for the townsfolk and summer visitors who walk and ride and picnic there. Unhappily the great drop from the thyme-scented turf of the cliff top to the sea pounding its base far below seems to have a morbidly irresistible attraction for a tragic few—for the actual and would-be suicides.

Originally the area was patrolled by a mounted civilian, but about 1930 this duty was taken over by the Eastbourne Police. That first constable and his successors have all been ex-Life or Horse Guardsmen, and have continued to be known by the old title of Downs Ranger. Mark, the first police horse, was stabled at a conveniently situated farm, but the next one, Tom, was moved to Beachy Head, to a disused RAF hut converted into a combined stable, police box, and store for rescue apparatus. After Tom died in 1949 it was decided to dispense with a Downs Ranger, but so many protests were made by both the public and the Town Council that three months later Princess Pat, a heavily built bay mare, arrived on the scene. Once more the Ranger set out on his patrols, and was replaced in 1953 when he retired.

The Downland Ranger's daily patrol lasts usually for three or four hours. During these lonely rides through the Sussex countryside, where the smell and sound of the sea are never entirely absent, man and his horse come to know their territory as well as an urban mounted policeman knows his city streets. When the swirling mists and sea fogs suddenly close down, reducing visibility to a yard or so in front of his horse's ears, the Ranger's knowledge comes into its own, both for his own safety and for that of the occasional stranger who loses his way, and is thankful for a friendly guide.

The Ranger is expected to cope with all and any occurrences that normally come the way of a policeman. In addition he must ride the many bridle and foot paths that criss-cross the downland and which, once obstructed, could cease to remain rights of way. He regularly visits the four or five farms in his area, and during the hard winter of 1963 when the farmhouses were completely cut off by huge snow drifts, Princess Pat carried essential supplies to them each day. On one occasion the mare trudged obediently through the snow, with a man each side holding a stirrup and another grasping her tail—guiding home a grateful trio who might well have been in real danger wandering in the bitter cold.

The potential suicides are one of the chief reasons for retaining a Downs Patrol. If the Ranger comes across one of these sad unfortunates, he does not dismount. This is a situation where once again a horse is an undisputed asset, where for some reason a man in the saddle seems to have a more calming effect than one on foot. The Ranger sits quietly talking while his horse champs the bit. The mere presence of this large, kindly looking animal with its understanding rider seems to radiate sympathy, and usually the person can be persuaded to accompany patrolman and horse back to the stable, for a cup of tea and a chat until the arrival of a patrol car relieves the Ranger of his responsibility.

When help arrives too late, or there has been an accident, or where some cliff climber's foolhardiness outruns his skill and rescue is necessary, the services of a Downs Patrol are always summoned. Through the years the Ranger inevitably gains an intimate knowledge of the cliffs themselves, from those that tower a sheer 500 feet above the beach, to those that have dwindled to chalky slopes and banks. His presence is a vital factor in any rescue attempt, and he always accompanies the operators of the equipment, the winch, 1,000 feet of cable and stretcher, to the site of the mishap.

Princess Pat became ill later in the winter of 1963 and was retired to a farm in Hampshire. In her rider's own words, 'She was never a good horse, but she had a wonderful personality, gentle as a lamb, very willing, and was a great favourite with the crowds of summer visitors.'

The seventeen-hands powerful grey gelding Jumbo who took her place is a distinct character, with one terrifying incident in his history to date. At first a rather nervous and difficult horse, he was just settling down in his new job when during a violent thunderstorm lightning struck the radio mast of the police box adjoining his stable. The stable windows were blown out, the electrical fittings destroyed and the building filled with smoke and dust. The Ranger, who was fortunately on the premises at the time, found his poor horse standing stock still, trembling violently. The gelding would neither eat nor drink for the next two days and was deaf through shock for three whole months, but his hearing gradually returned and he became more normal, if still nervous.

The new Ranger who took Jumbo on in 1966 has found him a gentle, playful horse, with a penchant for grabbing at coat buttons—a foible that accounts for dents in those of his master's uniform. At one time he used to mumble light switches until his stable was illuminated, and play with the handle of the inner stable door until it opened, and he could stretch his head round as far as the corn-bin. He put paid to this accomplishment, however, by biting off the door catch and incarcerating himself. Today the chief hazards to Jumbo come from the British public's extraordinary but friendly endeavours to feed every animal they come across with totally unsuitable food—the Downs Patrol horse's assortment of titbits including pork pies and sausage rolls!

The Glasgow police horses are so well acquainted with their city streets that any one of them left to his own devices in any part of the city centre would return his rider safely to the stables.

Horses do have this marked homing instinct, and it is a trait that can be used in more ways than one. Since—contrary to popular belief—policemen are human, it is inevitable that occasionally in severe weather a mounted constable will ride quietly down a back street to enjoy a cup of tea at the rear door of a restaurant, away from the public eye. It is suggested that an inquisitive superior, interested in knowing where these little irregularities occur, has only to take out the luckless constable's horse and ride him on a loose rein on his master's usual beat, to have the animal unknowingly play Judas! An illustration of this homing instinct was given by Prince, a twenty-year-old chestnut gelding of the Newcastle upon Tyne mounted section. Turned out to grass in the summer of 1960, in a field a mile from his stables, he promptly jumped the fence and returned to duty. Not to be coerced by insubordination, the police took him to another field, four miles away. For some days all was quiet, then a telephone call was received, announcing that Prince was at that moment threading his way through the High Street of a busy neighbouring town, en route to report for work. Since being retired to a horses' home in Norfolk, the reluctantly rusticated old chestnut appears to have accepted his discharge, and remains put.

In New York a police horse called Joseph escaped from his embarrassed rider one day and set off beneath the towering sky-scrapers of Manhattan for his stable. Unfortunately for Joseph he had forgotten that for some time he had had a new address. While a frantic patrolman was searching the environs of the stabling on 10th Street and 55th Avenue to no avail, a patient if puzzled Joseph was waiting hopefully by the non-existent door to his erstwhile, now-demolished stall on 94th Street and Madison Avenue.

CHAPTER FIVE

DUTY AMONGST THE SKYSCRAPERS

UNLIKE Joseph, Shawn did not live in New York although he too was a four-legged Rookie. He was a friendly six-year-old bay horse, not long up from a breeding farm in the countryside of Massachusetts, still a little amazed with city life, still learning his job. He had coped with his first assignment, duty near the Cathedral during a Red Mass, was finding it tempting to treat sewer and manhole covers as hazards to be jumped, and he had learned to ignore the fire-sirens that at first made him take off. He was a three-quarter-trained, as yet inexperienced police horse, who in 1959 inhabited one of the comfortable, deep-strawed stalls in the Back Bay Police Station, Boston—that New England city to which the *Mayflower* brought the Pilgrim Fathers in sixty-six storm-ridden days, as opposed to the modern traveller's seven-hour flight by jet.

Shawn, by now a veteran, may still see the haze rising over Beacon Hill, still carry his rider on patrol across Boston Common, where chickadees hop around the tub-thumpers on 'Speakers' Corner', as those happy orators hold forth on all and every subject just as their counterparts do in Hyde Park. His hooves may still thud on the paths separating the ornamental flower beds of the public garden, and he and his rider may yet circle the small lake where the return of the swans each year heralds the approaching spring; but if Shawn is operational today, he does not return to the Back Bay stables at the end of the day's work. That Station 16 closed in 1964, the mounted unit is located five miles away on a private estate in the Jamaica Plain section, and Sergeant Dooley, who schooled Shawn and all the other young police horses for so many years, has now retired. As he cannot bear to sever all connections with his charges, he keeps in touch by looking out for likely police mounts at horse shows and fairs, reporting any promising material to the lieutenant in command of the Boston Mounted Police.

Nowadays the section has been reduced to ten animals, but the unit is very much a going concern, and of recent years the horses have been used more and more often on crowd control. Time and again they have proved their ability to keep public demonstrations in hand, and the ability of one mounted man to replace a number of foot police. Fenway Park is the site of an Italian palace that a Mrs Gardner imported lock, stock and barrel in 1899, and set up as an art memorial to her husband. It is also where the exuberant fans of the Red Sox ball game queue for tickets. And when, a few years ago, an outsize crush at the ticket window grew to dangerous and disorderly proportions, four of the Boston mounted police were promptly available to show just how a trained horse can avert trouble. There are always several mounted policemen to be seen at the busy intersection of Summer and Winter Streets, right in the heart of the Boston shopping centre, their particular job in life being to discourage feather-brained and apparently suicide-intent pedestrians from launching themselves off the side-walk against the traffic-control lights. And whenever the city holds a parade the police horses lead the procession, partly to clear the streets, partly to add their natural dignity to the proceedings. They are there too, formed up in shining lines under the arc lights, at the start of a horse show at Boston Gardens; and for peeping over high fences to watch for signs of 'breaking and entering', what better position than the back of a horse? For patrolling the seven miles of wooded areas and trails within and adjoining the city, the horses have again firmly held their own against motor units.

These ten Boston horses are of course individuals, with different likes and dislikes, particularly when it comes to candy. Some enjoy eating cigarettes, and one or two, to their riders' confusion, have been known to lunch off a lady's straw hat. There is always the occasional horse who, faced with a yapping dog darting around its heels, throws manners to the winds and chases the little urchin! In the years just before and during the last war there was in fact a brown haired stable dog, Queenie, to prove that dog and horse can be friends. There was a goat as well, and even a monkey mascot that made the rounds of the stables, jumping from back to back of the horses as they stood in their stalls, and chattering with excitement when one or another enhanced the game by upending his heels. The horses were beautifully kept and beautifully schooled, just as they are today, and in the corral adjoining the stabling, Sergeant Dooley lunged and backed his charges, and taught them such refinements of manners as bowing, and stretching out to facilitate a rider mounting.

Like all police horses, temperament and conformation are of first importance, and the Boston station is not concerned with any particular breed, although bays and chestnuts are preferred in colour and the animals are always geldings. Before and during the war the horses ranged from the somewhat utility type of Amos to the fire and grace of Rusty, a striking little horse that must have been a descendant of the famous Justin Morgan— a stallion foaled in the Green Mountain country of Vermont in 1789 who reproduced his type with such exactness that it founded one of America's most famous general-purpose breeds, the Morgan. In fact Morgans by looks and temperament make good police horses, but are not often up to size. Justin Morgan only stood 14·2 hands, and the breed does not come over 15·1, added to which pure-bred Morgans are expensive. In Sergeant Dooley's days the Boston Police were lucky in possessing the friendship of a rich woman horse-lover, who would often help with the price of a particular animal when it was beyond the police allowance; owing to her generosity, from time to time an animal of Rusty's quality was acquired for the stables.

The Boston Police ride with leather 'overshoe' stirrups, and use the same 'spider rug', or shabrack under the saddle that, according to one New York Patrolman, can interfere with the leg aids. When snow rims the iron railings where riders once hitched their horses' reins, and which still stand around some of the nine-teenth-century houses in the vicinity of Beacon Hill, the police horses are well insulated, going on duty wearing smart woollen rugs that cover their bodies and strap across the chest. The horses are all ridden in the double Weymouth bridle and the Whiteman saddle, a cross between an English saddle and the American army McCullen.

There are no longer any cavalry horses in the USA but the 270 or so horses that police New York all wear saddles similar to the McCullen, with the same high cantle but with a lower, wider pommel. These saddles have the same centre vent as the army pattern, to relieve pressure on the horse's vertebrae—and which according to legend, was necessary during the military campaigns of bygone years to accommodate chargers so poor that their spines and ribs stuck out like those of a toastrack! The New York police horses also wear Weymouth bridles, with the emblem of the city police, first organised in 1664, mounted on the nearside of their browbands. A small plaque bearing the horse's name is attached to the cheekpiece and the animal's number is branded into the nearside hoof. A rope for hitching the horse while his rider eats is carried on the saddle. The patrolman is armed with a seldom-used pistol, handcuffs and a day or night stick, approximating to the British long truncheon. The night stick is the heavier, more formidable weapon, but whether this indicates that a tougher type of criminal is expected after dark is debatable.

In March 1967 a New York paper headlined its report on a Chicago conference: 'CURB ON WEAPONS OF POLICE URGED'. The report made reference to 'non-injurious weapons for the control and apprehension of most lawbreakers', and a representative called the police stick and gun 'obsolescent nineteenth-century' weapons, 'creating far worse problems than those the police are attempting to solve'. Tear-gas 'maces' were mentioned as an alternative, and these certainly give an additional method of riot control to the mounted policeman: recent tests have proved that, for some curious reason, horses are entirely unaffected by tear gas—and its use would seem preferable to that novel scheme evolved by a London Metropolitan Police horse, which sat down on a bicycle when on crowd control for the FA Cup Final at Wembley in May 1967!

In a few places in the world police horses may be kept on principally to enhance ceremonies, but this would never happen in New York. This city, as no other, epitomises modern times. The horses there do provide escorts for about a hundred parades every year, but sentiment and display alone would have short shrift amongst the crowding, pinkish-grey skyscrapers, amidst the rush and hustle of the traffic on those long avenues and crossing streets that make up the five boroughs of Greater New York. The city has grown up on a series of linked islands, with surrounding mosquito-ridden swamps, the unbelievable skyline created by buildings anchored on solid rock; it supports 8,000,000 people living in an area of 319 square miles, and is made up of 35,000 acres of park, 6,000 miles of street and 80 miles of waterfront. It has the largest mounted police force of any city in the world, and retains it because it is more efficient for certain jobs than any other method yet evolved. Apart from other considerations, the horses and the men who ride them are on excellent terms with the public, an advantage not always enjoyed by the tough New York cops working on foot or with motor vehicles.

The Mounted District is divided amongst a number of squadrons. On traffic-control duty in Manhattan, the horse's ability to back, an essential instilled during training, is heavily tested amongst the packed vehicles. The horses also patrol Riverside, Bronx and Brooklyn, and during the summer some of them are moved from the business areas to parks and to beaches like Coney Island. One of the mounted policeman's toughest assignments, calling for the most experienced men and the steadiest horses, is the congested Garment area. On streets thick with heavy traffic, thieves nimbly filch bolts of cloth from parked trucks, often those waiting to make deliveries. The driver of a police car might possibly be able to stand up and see, and be seen, for as many blocks as a patrolman on his horse, but in an emergency he can scarcely manoeuvre his car up over the curb, to get through the conglomeration and give chase, as the horseman will.

In Central Park, a haven of birds and squirrels, trees and blossom, which only a little over one hundred years ago was a 'bare, unsightly and disgusting spot', the mounted patrolmen's hours of duty more or less follow the sun—a 10-till-6 shift all the year round with an additional one, 5 pm to 1 am, from April until fall. A park patrol can produce anything from stopping a runaway horse on a bridle path to capturing a rapist; murders are not unknown, and the patrolman may have the gruesome job of guarding a corpse, or the relatively light-hearted one of galloping after a purse-snatcher, or—far more often—just keeping people on the move along the paths. The park has its quota of 'characters' and although these are mostly not of criminal intent, even the best-trained police horse may be excused for taking exception to a punchdrunk fighter shadow-boxing round a tree, or some oddity lying prone, doing setting-up exercises (press-ups) in the dark.

The notorious gangsters of the past are no longer a major problem, yet New York's reputation for crime is not exaggerated, any more than the musical *West Side Story* strays far from the truth. Nowadays the most pressing police anxiety is the one that menaces so many countries, the increase in the use of narcotics. Addicts craving for a drug, or for the money to buy it, will lose normal inhibitions about law-breaking. The presence, or potential presence, of a mounted policeman is in New York, as anywhere else, a strong crime deterrent. When men and horses leave their regular patrols, it is nearly always to supervise a crowd, whether it comprises a waterfront riot or a bargain sale. During the United Nations General Assembly meeting in 1960, for instance, the attendance of Mr Khruschev and Fidel Castro, among other world notabilities, kept more than 200 men and horses patrolling the Manhattan area for eight hours a day; and a task force was several times sent to Harlem to deal with Castro's high-spirited supporters.

The New York police horses have their share of accidents, but most of these arise from slipping up on manhole covers or wet pavements, or from sudden shying. Even the most reliable horse can occasionally spook at a street-cleaning machine with its rotating brushes, or get upset by the loose canvas on a passing truck, and shy into the glass in front of a dress platform. Considering the density of traffic in the city, the reason that more police horses are not hit by cars may be that motorists know that a patrolman will dismount, and write out an on-the-spot summons for a careless driver who comes too close.

New York's Mounted Police began in 1871, with a squad consisting of a sergeant, twelve patrolmen, a hostler and fifteen horses. It was formed for the purpose of dealing with 'a certain class of persons' who, since the avenues to and beyond Central Park had been laid with smooth pavements and become crowded with vehicles, had begun 'fast and reckless driving . . . at rates of speed perilous to the lives and property of themselves and more prudent and orderly citizens.' The Mounted Squad No. 1 was responsible for Fifth, Sixth and Seventh Avenues, from Fourteenth Street to Fifty-ninth, and Lexington Avenue from Fourteenth to Thirty-fourth. They were so successful in reducing the casualties and injuries and guarding the interests of the more orderly, that the avenues in question could then be used 'with a degree of comfort and safety not hitherto enjoyed'. Within a few years these mounted patrolmen, capable of covering three times as much ground as a man on foot, were distributed over a wider area. A training stable and school of instruction was established in 1899, by which time there were 385 police horses, 230 used on mounted patrol and the remainder in harness.

That same year the mounted police evolved a tactic for dealing with large crowds which is still taught, and occasionally used. In the fall of 1899, New York gave Admiral George Dewey, returning from the Spanish-American war, a hero's welcome : there was never before 'assembled in any city for any occasion of the kind, such a large crowd.' The Chief of Police deployed his men and horses in the form of a wedge or triangle, preceded by 'four roundsmen (sergeants) and fifteen patrolmen as skirmishers'. With an officer in front, two riders behind him and five more lines of patrolmen, increasing by two per line, back to the 'base' of twelve that fills the breadth of the street, the 'flying wedge' can move into the heart of a crowd and split it into two. The effectiveness of this manoeuvre was demonstrated in 1961 when a huge crowd at the United Nations, protesting at the death

of Patrice Lumumba, set off for Times Square through the thick
of rush-hour traffic. Mounted police using the 'flying wedge'
managed to stop the marchers, without serious injury to anyone,
before they reached Broadway.

By 1910 the Police Department owned 724 horses, but the
numbers gradually decreased from the next year, in proportion to
the increase in the horseless petrol-wagons, first tried in 1911. In
1919 an outbreak of riots, strikes and post-war parades brought
plenty of police work; a memorable job for the horses was
preventing a serious disturbance when servicemen attempted to
storm the Lexington Opera House where a German opera was
scheduled. They coped with similar trouble in 1939, when protesting groups beseiged a rally held in Madison Square by the
German-American Bund. Between the world wars the mounties
had been kept busy with crowd control occasioned by the
arrival of heads of States from abroad, St Patrick's Day parades
and American Legion conventions. Nowadays both men and
horses can be transported anywhere they are needed by vans, big
horse-boxes where the animals, wearing muzzles, stand head to
tail, four each side.

After world war II the mounted police were again cut in
numbers, partly because it was not easy to come by the right
type of horse, partly owing to problems of stabling. To a degree
these difficulties remain today, although the strength of the force
is now static. In the old days most of the horses came from
Kentucky and Ohio, and later from Kansas City, but the type
of animal the police require gets yearly scarcer, and nowadays
most come from further west, from the Dakotas, Wyoming or
Saskatchewan. As the potential London Metropolitan police
horses are collected for inspection in Yorkshire, known dealers
and cattlemen muster likely animals in corrals to be looked over
by the New York Police buying committee. Even so the committee may return three or four short of the twenty or so remounts
that are required each year. They look for four-to-six-year-old
bay geldings, sound in wind and limb, good movers and up to
weight. The horses have to be intelligent, kindly animals, 15.3 to

16.2 hands high, with quality and good conformation, long manes and tails, and sound feet, not so big that the animal is clumsy-footed. The majority of these horses arrive from the west shaggy, rough, unaccustomed alike to pavements to walk on or oats to eat, and many suffering from 'shipping sickness'—a kind of equine distemper which fortunately reacts quickly to penicillin. They are all on ten days' probation, and during that time are given the most stringent of veterinary tests. Those that are finally chosen go through a normal training, which takes about six months. After only a few weeks it is almost impossible to recognise the nervous, wild-eyed, rough-coated intakes in the rounded, sleek and quiet-mannered creatures undergoing training.

The horses are of mixed American breeds. Some, like Rusty of Boston, show Morgan characteristics. Richard, the eleven-year-old ridden by the captain of Troop C, is a good-looking thoroughbred type, and a frequent performer in musical rides and in jumping exhibitions at the Madison Square Garden Horse Show in the fall. Jordan and Watson, both good horses in the same troop, are half-brothers from an Indian reservation. Troop C has the usual quota of characters amongst its horses; Saxa, an excellent patrol horse but nervous in the stable and inclined to kick; Rival, one of the few that wears a martingale because, according to his rider, 'he just loves dressing up—if he was a woman he'd wear cheap jewellery'; and the inevitable 'difficult' animal that was just looking for a rider to suit and has now found one. The men draw a veil over the activities of Patriarch; he chews tails, and is a sore subject with one or two patrolmen who have to ride horses owning only half this decorative appendage.

The problem of stabling remains acute. Troop C is based on an ex-cab garage on 10th Avenue and 55th Street. The fifty-five horses are kept in stalls with blue paintwork and thick straw beds, two loose-boxes being available for any sick animal. These are palatial quarters compared with those of the sixty-five horses living on the second and third floors of an eighty-one-year-old waterfront stable. Built in the last century for wagon horses belonging to junk dealers and fruit pedlars, it lacks heating, a big consideration in a city where the night temperatures in winter can be fiercely cold; rain drips into the saddle-room and high tide washes the cellar. Worse still, the whole building is a potential fire trap, with thick beamed wooden floors and a dark exit ramp to the street, with room for only one horse at a time. Horses panic in smoke, and a fire in those stables could not only lead to the deaths of animals whose welfare the patrolmen place far above their own, but could bring an irreplaceable loss to the Police Department. It may only take six or seven months to train a horse sufficiently to go out on patrol, but it is five years before the animal can be considered fully developed and knowledgeable. There are hopes that new stabling for 150 horses will be built at Central Park, underground so that the view and amenities remain unspoilt. The idea is to include police stables, public stables, and two large rings with seats for spectators, where horses could be trained and exercised.

As with all mounted police forces the men who used to make up the New York squadrons were ex-cavalrymen. Nowadays, as with the British mounted policemen, few have ridden before. The young men are selected volunteers from other police departments, and are taught on much the same lines as those employed at Imber Court, and by much the same type of dedicated rider. The horses used for training have just as much fun with the rookies as their counterparts have back in England. One will take a short gallop for no apparent reason, with its unfortunate rider bouncing up and down and imploring his mount to take it easy, which it then does—without warning; another will cart a novice to the entrance gate and refuse to leave until the officer in charge of the school comes to the rescue. Then, in an astonishingly short while, the men begin to get the hang of it, and almost before they realise the fact themselves their horses, being horses, will be behaving as though butter not only will not melt, but has never melted in their mouths. The training is strenuous and intensive, and the men all have to learn to ride in a uniform manner, with military seat, and the stirrup on the ball of the foot. They have first to learn how to ride on the snaffle bit, the bridoon, and then master the use of the curb for street duty. Eventually they will

'Nuisance Training'. It takes a lot to shift a police horse!

Horses of the City of Salford mounted branch on park patrol (above)

Edinburgh's crowds controlled by some of the City's police horses (left)

A smart contingent from Newcastle upon Tyne (below)

discover that by 'collecting' a horse properly between hands and legs it is possible to exploit his natural reaction of excitement to bands and crowds, and make him arch his neck, show his teeth and flare his nostrils, putting on an apparently fierce appearance which can help materially in stopping a fight or controlling a riot.

When the London Metropolitan Police horses have reached the end of their working life, they are humanely destroyed. This does not apply to gift horses, which are returned to their owners, and was a decision taken only to save horses from being deprived of the meticulous care and attention which they have received for so many years. New York horses are all sent on retirement to the Health Department's pleasant farm at Otisville, where they are carefully looked after and make their contribution by providing blood serum for diphtheria and tetanus antitoxins. In Iran, mules and old horses, some from the mounted police force of Teheran, are used for the same purpose at the magnificent Razi Institute at Karaj.

CHAPTER SIX

IRANIAN STALLIONS AND
THE DESERT PATROL

TO the north, beyond the sprawling tree-decked city that is Teheran, beyond the wide, motor-traffic filled avenues of the modern city, the narrow streets of the older parts where horse-drawn droshkys still ply for trade, and laden, bridleless donkeys patter by with a seemingly inborn traffic sense, the tremendous rock barrier of the Elburz mountains rears up against a cloudless sky, the range dominated by the snow-capped conical peak of Demavend.

My husband and I had opportunity for studying these mountains from afar, as we sat patiently in our official car outside the largest sports stadium in Teheran, a colossal amphitheatre with seating for 20,000 people. Around us pushed and chattered and shouted a milling horde of excited Iranians, all bent on filling those seats to capacity, but excluded for the moment by tall iron gates and the concerted efforts of stalwart Teheran foot police. Unfortunately for us the crowd's fixed resolve to get inside willy-nilly excluded ourselves as well, official invitation or no, and so we waited, talking over the magnificent events of the morning.

We had been up early to arrive on time at the glittering, fabulous royal museum and treasure house that is the Gorleston Palace. We were ushered up a stairway, carpeted with the traditional Persian patterns in reds and blues and greens, and lined to either hand with a detachment of the Imperial Guard, resplendent in ceremonial uniforms and plumed helmets. We made our way past panels of priceless mosaics, depicting hunting scenes of centuries ago and still glowing with that indescribable,

indestructible shade of blue that is the colour of Iran, to a vast
ante-room.

Next door in the Hall of Mirrors, His Imperial Majesty
Mohammed Reza Shah Pahlavi was receiving the greetings and
congratulations of his ministers, officials and service chiefs, and of
the foreign ambassadors and diplomats gathered at the Palace for
the Salaam Ceremony, an integral part of the annual celebrations
for His Imperial Majesty's birthday. The ante-room had been
seething with figures in diplomatic and morning dress, with
splendid personages in bright uniforms ornamented with gold
braid and heavy with decorations, and here and there with a
Sheikh from some Arab state, gliding by in his gold-sewn
burnous. Outside the windows that stretched from embossed
ceiling to Persian-carpeted floor, a colourful pageant of those on
their way to the ceremony paused beside an ornamental pool to
enjoy the shade of the trees, while a band played and roses
bloomed in the scented air.

Now, however, we were still on the wrong side of the stadium
gates, and looked like remaining there. Each time the police
cleared a gap in front of our car and started to ease open the
barrier, the crowd made a boisterous and unified rush that made
our passage impossible, and gave the police no little trouble in
closing the gap once more. Then, suddenly and miraculously, we
were inside. One moment the people were pressing round us in
a solid phalanx that threatened to cave in the sides of the car, the
next moment there was space to move and most of the crowd
seemed to have vanished. I looked back to find the origin of this
miracle, and saw the pricked ears and fiery beauty of half a
dozen stallions ridden to the scene by a section of the Teheran
Mounted Police force.

A few days later we were to meet these horses again, amongst
the 120 or so animals stabled at the mounted police depot. We
were taken into the dim, cool stables, where the horses, all
stallions, are tethered in long lines facing each other across a
gangway. There is little in the way of a partition between
each horse, a heel-rope on one hind leg providing the necessary
anchor.

The horses are of different breeds and cross-breeds, but are all country-bred of Persian origin, and possess the stamina, high courage and spirited temperaments that automatically go with the horses of this huge and fascinating land. Many of them are Turkomans, those fine animals bred by the semi-nomadic tribes living in the wide desert to the north-east of Iran, close up to the Russian border. The oldest and purest type of Turkoman horse is that called an Akhal Tekeh. It is an interesting comment on the man-made barriers between different countries that the Russians also have a similar, equally fine breed of horse, coming from the other side of that Turkoman border—in fact Prince Philip was given a Russian Akhal Tekeh stallion by Mr Khruschev and Marshal Bulganin in 1956, and the horse, Mele-Kush, is still a cherished inmate of the Royal Mews at Windsor.

In the Royal Mews at Farahabad, on the outskirts of Teheran, it is easy to pick out the Turkoman horses from the magnificent Persian Arab, Darashoori and other breeds by their lack of mane; it is traditional to hog these horses once they are sold away from the desert regions of their birth. All the Teheran police horses, Turkoman or not, have hogged manes like the pre-first world war Metropolitan animals, which had clipped manes as well as short-ened tails. As better-bred horses were gradually introduced into the London force the practice was stopped, but the manes of the good-class Teheran police horses are sacrificed in the cause of greater cleanliness in a hot country.

The mounted police are planning to build a riding school. They already possess a good-sized exercising manège where the going is very different from the rough, dry and stony ground over which, once off the city streets, Persian horses have perforce to work, and which is largely the cause of the prevalent hoof and tendon troubles. The horses are well schooled and well ridden, but very active and mettlesome and, after watching them and riding a couple for myself, I can well understand why the crowd outside the sports stadium preferred discretion to valour! The majority of the stallions in the Middle East are remarkably well behaved. Their manners of course depend to a large extent on how they are treated, but a good temperament is characteristic of the

Arabian horse, and the stallions, instead of being kept solely for breeding purposes, are worked much as geldings are in Britain. With the exception of the horses belonging to the Imperial Guard in Iran, few in the Middle East are gelded. On the big estates it is the mares that are kept solely for breeding. There was, however, a moment of drama when we asked four of the policemen to ride towards us in close formation for a photograph. Too polite to refuse the request of a guest, there seemed to be a certain unease amongst the men as well as their horses, and as they rode forwards their ranks gradually widened until they were beyond the range of our camera. I had forgotten that, with the exception of the Shah's beautifully mannered animals, few stallions can be ridden close to each other without the risk of a fight.

The police horses here are all black, bay or chestnut, the preference for darkish colouring lying in the nature of their work. The mounted police in addition to their heavy load of crowd and traffic control, and of special duties when heads of other states are visiting Teheran, patrol the streets of the city for four or five hours each night. And along the broad, shadowy boulevards, lined with tall, aromatic-leaved plane trees that grow in irrigation channels on either side, a grey or light-coloured horse would be too conspicuous.

By way of relaxation for man and beast, and when work allows, the police race their horses during the season, and take part in any local displays. They are keen to take a larger part in show-jumping and other competitions in the future, and are gradually training up the young intake of horses for this purpose —not always an easy task when it comes to jumping, because of the Persian horses' natural propensity to be impetuous and excitable.

The Teheran mounted police wear smart navy-blue uniforms, blue or black ties, black boots and blue, white-banded fibre-glass helmets—which have a steel shell to fit over the top in emergencies. On their saddles they carry a sword to their right hand, a rifle to their left, unaccustomed impedimenta to me, in which I managed to get entangled when mounting. We were given a mock demonstration of firing from the saddle, a different drill from that practised by the New York mounted police who, on the rare occasions they discharge their .38 calibre revolvers, dismount first. These Teheran stallions are trained to gunfire and stood like rocks, while their riders demonstrated how they hold the reins beneath the rifle.

The horses wear standard bits similar to the army universal pelhams in use in Britain, and the saddles too are standard army type. They have a raised cantle but are not as high as those Persian hunting saddles which, built up fore and aft of the rider, are the most comfortable and safest form of tack imaginable, especially when riding on the shaly, precipitous moufflon trails that wind up and down the Elburz range. Their saddle cloths bear the insignia of the Police Department of Iran.

In Jordan, the tanned, wiry men who ride the stone and sand deserts policing the country's long, arid borders to the north-east and south, wear their police badge on the centre of the black cord 'agal' that keeps in place the red-and-white check-ered shemagh, the same headdress as that of the Royal Jordanian Army. It is not in fact always easy to tell where the Jordanian army ends and the police begin. Both have tenuous roots in that Arab army which under the Emir Feisal and Lawrence of Arabia rose against the Turks during the first world war.

In 1921 the Amir Abdullah, the grandfather of the present King Hussein of Jordan, accepted the sovereignty of the then newly formed state called Trans-Jordan: a country of which four-fifths was desert, inhabited by the nomadic, lawless Bedouin. Before their overthrow the Turks had had some control over the villagers in the far north, but had not attempted the near-impossible task of subjugating the greater part of the desert, and the tribes had not been subjected to any real form of government for centuries. The Amir's administration organised a police force, but it was scarcely large enough to cope with three provincial towns and the new capital, Amman, let alone the Bedouin.

Two Englishmen were instrumental in bringing eventual peace to the desert: Captain (later Lt-Col) Peake, who arrived in

Trans-Jordan in the early days to assist the Amir Abdullah in forming an army, the renowned Arab Legion, and the man who came to be known throughout the length and breadth of the country as Glubb Pasha, or Abu Haneik, Lt-General Sir John Glubb. He became Peake's successor, until he left the country in 1956, and was the organiser of the original Desert Patrol, an offshoot of the Legion.

Soon after the inception of the Arab Legion, the 300-strong police force of Trans-Jordan was put under the same command. Some years later, owing to various complex treaties negotiated within the more-than-complex politics of the Middle East, British imperial troops of the Trans-Jordan Frontier Force for a while took over the defence of the country against outside aggression, while the Arab Legion was responsible for internal security and the duties of the gendarmerie. During world war II the bulk of the Legion reverted to its purely military role, and throughout the Middle East the exploits of the Arab Legion were acclaimed as second to none.

Up to 1931, in common with most other Arabian desert regions, those east of the Jordan river, up to the Syrian and Saudi-Arabian frontiers, remained areas of bloodshed, violence and feud. The Bedouin tribes continued their age-old pastime of raiding each other, and the few travellers journeyed at their peril. To add to the dangers and confusion, all through the early and middle 1920s and again in 1930, warriors of the fanatical religious sect, the Wahhabi Movement, were marauding across the border from Saudi Arabia, bent on instilling stricter Muslim principles by the sword. As often as not the target of the Ikhwan, the Brethren as they were called, was the big Bedouin tribe of Huwaitet; and the Ikhwan's inapposite war cry, 'La Illaha ill Allah—There is no God but God' came to be dreaded as on surprise raids they slaughtered men, women and children alike, carrying off flocks of camels, sheep and goats as booty.

Largely owing to their inaccessibility, and because they themselves were mobile on camels, the Bedouin remained independent of government control until motor vehicles began to penetrate their desert fastness, and taxes and other impedimenta of their country's law began to appear on the horizon of their lives. Innately suspicious of any government and, owing to mutual misunderstandings, equally mistrustful of the British troops trying to promote peace along the Saudi-Arabian frontier, the Bedouin continued to ignore such government officials as reached them, and the Huwaitet continued to try remedying their losses at the hands of the Ikhwan by retaliatory raids into Saudi Arabia.

Such was the chaotic position in the desert when Glubb Pasha arrived, commissioned with the unenviable tasks of recruiting a desert police force of ninety men, and putting an end, once and for all, to inter-tribal raiding. Concentrating first on the most critical Huwaiti area, he achieved his object there and all over the Jordan desert by using a mixture of strategy, applied psychology and, eventually, mutual goodwill. The tribes acknowledged the force of the argument that if they did not police themselves others would be imported to do so, and a trickle of recruits grew to a long waiting list for the ranks of the Desert Patrol and Arab Legion—Bedouin herdsmen who have proved themselves some of the finest soldiers in the world. Within a miraculously short time the Bedouin ceased entirely to raid each other, travellers journeyed in safety, and the Desert Patrol was able to concentrate on the same police-cum-army duties it performs today.

The Camel Corps is the crack police corps of the Desert Patrol. Although motor vehicles did much to pacify the desert, camels can still travel over terrain and cope with conditions that would be uneconomic or impassable for cars, and impossible for horses, even for the nimble little Arabians used by the Jordan gendarmerie. The Camel Corps use the élite, well-bred, speedy single-humped Arabian dromedaries, as unlike the lumbering two-humped baggage camels of Asia, or the hard-worked all-purpose beasts of the Bedouin, as racehorses are unlike heavy cart breeds. The Corps operates from the north-east, down through the Suwwan or Flinty Deserts, where the camels callouse their knees as they fold up grumbling amongst the stones, to the sandy wastes and magnificent rock djebels of the Wadi Rumm, where they shuffle the burning sand away as they kneel. They patrol the borders with Syria and Saudi Arabia, on the look-out for smugglers, opium dealers and other undesirables attempting illegal entry into Jordan. Often these characters are also mounted on camels, and since the only sign of their presence may be a small dust-cloud on the horizon, the speed of the Corps animals is fully used.

The picturesque outposts of the desert police are scattered at intervals all over the eastern desert. Small forts with thick white walls punctuated with gun slits, built on a square with a squat look-out tower, massive iron doors as an entrance and a camel-compound outside. Inside, the courtyard is shady with trees and adorned with flower-beds watered by a sprinkler, the men's quarters and store-rooms grouped round with the added essentials of armoury and radio-room.

The patrols, usually of four men and camels, operating from these forts may be away from base for some days at a time. The riders wear a decorative but practical uniform of long-skirted khaki tunic over white trousers and checked shemagh—that headdress which, with the civilian version, the keffiya, is the most practical and versatile of all desert head-coverings. Crossed bandoliers and a silver-clasped belt are studded with cartridges for the rifle slung behind, and with ammunition for the colt revolver worn on one thigh. A curved dagger in a silver scabbard hanging in front completes the desert policeman's arms, and red tassels here and there for decoration add to the overall romantic if efficient effect.

On patrol, the camel's rations of barley and alfalfa are carried in a bag behind the saddle. One blanket goes underneath the saddle, and others are stowed with the remainder of the equipment in two capacious brightly embroidered saddle-bags. For winter work, when the desert can be lashed by rain-squalls as well as being wickedly cold, two plastic-covered rugs are carried, one for the camel and one for its rider, identical except for size and the hump-containing hole in one of them. By night the patrol, taking turn about with a two-hour sentry trick, sleep rolled head and all in scarlet woollen cloaks, their rifles to hand, beside their folded up, cud-chewing beasts. They lie on the boulder-strewn, flinty surface, beneath an immensity of stars that once seen can never be forgotten.

The camels wear tightly fitting coloured headstalls, with a running chain under the chin that comes to the rider's hand as a single, brightly coloured rope. Impetuous beasts have an extra rope attached to the side of one nostril, but a camel is steered by light taps applied to either side of its neck plus admonitions in Arabic—not by the single 'rein'—as I discovered when I pulled it and my camel began an ominous and terrifying buckling of the legs. The saddles are well padded, with a goatskin for added comfort, secured with soft rope girths and with a slim wooden upright fore and aft. Once having experienced the eruptive actions of a camel both getting up and kneeling down, the necessity of these hand anchors is appreciated.

Camels are one of the most perfectly evolved creatures for their particular environment in the world. If necessary they can feed off the sparse desert scrub and can go up to ten days without water. Their two-toed, spongy feet adapt to the unspeakably flinty surfaces of the Suwwan as well as to yielding sand; they can close their nostrils, and veil their eyes with long film-star lashes, to keep out the stinging sand and stifling dust of storms; and though, like all of their kind, they growl and grumble and protest, the animals of the Camel Corps are instantly obedient to their riders' commands. The djemels, the males, incline to bite and are dangerous during the rut, and no one, least of all a European, should try patting a camel of either sex as he would a horse. Like aeroplanes, these animals need a long runway to gather speed, at any rate on rough surfaces, but once under way they can out-gallop a horse. Whatever their few drawbacks, it will be a sad day if the Camel Corps in Jordan ever takes to a mechanical version of its ships of the desert.

All over the Jordan countryside are dotted the posts of the gendarmerie, the ex-farmers, soldiers-cum-policemen, the universal guides, philosophers and friends of the rural Jordanian people, who throughout the Palestinian troubles of 1936-9 and through nearly six years of the last world war, kept the peace of the Trans-

Jordan countryside undisturbed. During the war the Amir
Abdullah sent every available soldier to the help of Britain and
her allies, and not one had to be diverted from war service to
maintain internal order. In those days the gendarmerie all rode
the quick, beautiful Arabian horses of their land, but nowadays
most of them are motorised. There are however some who still
find horses the best mode of transport, as I discovered when I
visited that mounted patrol of the Jerusalem police beside the
Jericho road, where I watched a sergeant groom his horse in the
traditionally British manner.

Most of these horses are not of the valuable old blood lines,
like those lovely creatures of 'dished' profiles and huge eyes to be
seen at King Hussein's stud at Shuna, near the Dead Sea, though
occasionally Mr Santiago, the Royal Horsemaster, spots a mare
of ancient lineage amongst them—such as Shammah, a grey
police mare now at Shuna, who is by Seglawi Sherifi, a stallion of
an almost extinct line that belonged to the Amir, later King,
Abdullah. The majority of the police horses today are native-
bred, wiry, attractive little Arabian animals, capable of carrying
a policeman for hours on end over the unspeakable going of the
stony deserts. Unlike the Iranian police, those of Jordan ride
mares, keeping the stallions for breeding purposes and as riding
animals for personages of note.

The police post at the Inn of the Good Samaritan is supplied
from Jerusalem, and linked by radio to the headquarters there.
The horses are fed three times daily on barley, with alfalfa at
mid-day and evening to supply bulk. Like the Bedouin, who
consider that desert horses should be deliberately trained to go
without water, the police here water the horses three times a day
in summer, but only twice in winter. Those that I saw were tacked
out in saddles and bridles of British army pattern, and all four
mares appeared somewhat frightened of their mouths—no doubt
because many of their riders are Bedouin police recruits, men
who grew up riding the horses of their tribe on bitless headstalls
with a single rope, and who have an understandable indifference
to the rider's art of 'hands'.

The duties of these patrols range from collecting and making a census of livestock, to taking messages to some remote village or a summons to one of the black, goats-hair tents of the Bedouin. They are expected to deal with general public security and to keep the peace. Sometimes they set out to apprehend a criminal and may indulge in real cloak-and-dagger stuff, with two men on ahead in disguise and the third to bring up the horses when required. They carry rifles, and well know how to use them, and when they ride by night, finding their way with the help of the stars, their quick-moving little horses make as light of the harsh ground as they do by day.

Before leaving the police patrol at the Inn of the Good Samaritan, I went into the guardroom to fetch my tape-recorder. It was cool inside and very tidy. An oil lamp threw a pool of light amongst the shadows, and through the doorway, beyond the rim of the wall containing the compound, the dark hills stretched away, range upon range, arid, rocky and compelling, to where the last faint streaks of light stained the night sky. Between the two world wars and during the last one, there were British policemen, both mounted and on foot, in that controversial Holy Land lying west of the river Jordan.

The Palestine Police, a civil force, came into being mainly because Lawrence's assurances to the Arabs, given in good faith to the Emir Faisal, were not in the end implemented by the British Government. At the conclusion of the Great War the Palestinian Arabs had cause for believing that the Emir Faisal, with his Arab Army, would become their ruler. Instead, the British established a League of Nations mandate for the country, and on the basis of the Balfour Declaration of 1917 a territorial home for the Jews began to build up in a land to which the resident Arabs equally laid claim. Policemen are not concerned with politics, but the men and horses of the Palestine Police had the difficult task of endeavouring to keep the peace between the two factions—while the Arabs' bitterness grew stronger with each influx of Jews from all over the world.

After world war II there was no longer a League of Nations, mandates had become obsolete, and the United Nations endeavoured to contend with Great Britain's two mandated territories in the Middle East. Trans-Jordan became wholly independent under King Abdullah, and Palestine was divided into three, an Arab area, the Jewish area which as Israel is still unacknowledged in Arab countries, and an international zone consisting of Jerusalem and other Holy Places sacred alike to Moslem, Christian and Jew. As soon as it was known that the British were to pull out of Trans-Jordan, spasmodic fighting flared up between Arabs and Jews, culminating in the short-lived Arab-Israeli war, which broke out on the day the British mandate finally expired, 15 May 1948. The bitter fighting ended in an uneasy, always dangerous and never-ratified truce, and on the transformation of Trans-Jordan into Jordan.

Several members of the present-day Mounted Section of the Metropolitan Police in London came from the Palestine Police, after that force was disbanded with the end of the British mandate. Now these men patrol the London streets for three hours a day, work wholly different from the duties in the Holy Land.

It was an exciting, interesting life not without danger. They carried arms, and rode for miles into the Palestine countryside, visiting Arab villages and Jewish settlements. A patrol never lasted less than a day, sometimes stretching into days on end and occasionally into weeks. The men had to be able to speak both Arabic and Hebrew, they shared the food of the Arabs and by night slept with their horses in Arab villages. There were many incidents like that on a night in November 1945 when the Jews attacked the coastguard station at Sidna Ali with automatic weapons, rifles and grenades. There was sharp fighting between the attackers and the small garrison of Palestinian mounted police and Arabs, and the building was damaged by explosions before the attackers eventually withdrew. Five British and five Arabs were slightly wounded, but all the horses escaped injury.

During the last war men were released from the army to serve in the Palestine Police, being placed on a class of army reserve, and retaining an equivalent rank.

CHAPTER SEVEN

AUSTRALIAN TROOPER
POLICE HORSES

AMONGST the many overseas contributors to a News Letter
run by the Palestine Police Old Comrades' Association
are members who sought careers in Australia after the
Palestine Police broke up. They joined different branches of a
force with a long and tough tradition, closely interwoven with
Australia's growth.

It was not until 1770 that Captain Cook landed at Botany Bay
and formally took possession of New South Wales in the name
of Britain's King George III. Nor was there then any rush to
settle the vast tracts of this new land, where the savannah of the
tropical north turns to the tall, dense eucalyptus forests of the
east coasts and southern corners; where scrubby thickets of mulga
and mallee fringe those areas of the south-west which are arid
desert; and where the brilliant light falls alike on the blues and
greys and reddish-browns of a vegetation sharply contrasting
with the lush green of English trees. Nations were ready to own
new lands in which to establish trading posts and naval bases,
but there was no general belief in the value of colonies. Britain
had for years been contending with the troubles attendant on
holding America as a colony, troubles that burst into the
American War of Independence only five years after Captain
Cook's landing. It was this American Revolution, combined with
the beginnings of the economic revolution in England and the
crime and criminal laws of the time, that eventually provided the
first, involuntary, 'settlers' in Australia.

In Britain the population was increasing fast, and owing to
famine and high prices thousands of people were uprooted from

the villages, and crowded into the tenements and overrun alleys of the towns where, Fielding observed, 'They starve and freeze and rot amongst themselves, but they beg and steal and rob amongst their betters.' The savagery of the criminal law rose in ratio to the increasing incidence of crime, but without any deterrent effect. The prisons and hulks were overflowing, and convicts could no longer be transported to the American colonies. In the beginning, Australia appeared as a heaven-sent overflow for the prison population, and in 1788 the first transports carrying almost 1,500 people moored in Sydney Cove. The transportation of criminals to New South Wales continued until 1840, and in all about 160,000 people arrived in Australia as convicts. The deathroll in the ships that brought them was appalling, and they suffered unspeakably in penal settlements such as Port Arthur and Norfolk Island, where a convict might be sent for felonies committed after his arrival.

The majority of them were assigned work in gangs for building and road making. Those who became assigned servants remained at the whim of their masters, but in some cases were no worse off, at any rate for food, than rural labourers back in England. The transportation system was a savage atrocity, but it provided a motive for settlement, and a supply of cheap labour for the free immigrants who followed on. It was by no means the worst offenders who were transported to Australia. As Lord John Russell declared, 'A man is estimated by his capacity as a colonist; not by his crime as a felon,' and a House of Commons Committee reported that, 'The previous occupation of a convict in this country mainly determines his condition in the penal colonies.' In time the convicts became free, either by expiry or remission of their sentences; a few became wealthy merchants and professional men, the majority lived as farmers, artisans, shopkeepers, labourers and shepherds. Not until around 1815 were many free settlers anxious to emigrate to Australia.

At the beginning of the nineteenth century the military struggled to keep some form of law and order in most of the settled areas of the continent and the different States gradually, at varying times, achieved some form of policing, however

haphazard. In New South Wales a few semi-civilians had been
tried out to supplement and succeed the army police, but it was
1811 before the State acquired its first superintendent of constables. Then, in 1825, four years before Sir Robert Peel's
Metropolitan Police Acts gave London its first Bobbies, and
around the time that Britain's notorious highwaymen quitted the
scene, Governor Brisbane of New South Wales drafted Australia's
first patrol of mounted police. Intended principally to protect the
settlers from horse and cattle stealing, a patrol with mobility was
obviously necessary, especially as the colony expanded west of
the upthrust blocks of the Blue Mountains and up the Hunter
River valley.

The patrol consisted of two officers and thirteen troopers, or
Trooper Police, as they were called, and was semi-military both
in character and looks. Recruited mainly from infantry regiments serving in the colony, the men wore a dress uniform, a
jacket with white facings, blue pants with a white stripe and a
peakless cap, very similar to that of a regiment of Light Dragoons,
and carried a sabre, carbine and horse-pistols. The sword was
dispensed with in the bush, and their bush or working dress consisted of a patrol jacket and trousers and what is known as a
'cabbage tree' or leghorn hat, sometimes decorated with a green
veil as protection against mosquitoes.

From the start this small force found an exacting job on their
hands dealing with the bushrangers. These were ex-convicts who
retained an ineradicable criminal taint, or men driven to flight by
the brutalities in the roadmaking gangs or under the lash of
a tyrannical master. They took to the wild terrain that crept to
the town doorsteps, to the heat and dust of the sun-baked earth
and the sudden rush of rank grass after the 'wet', when a mud-
choked gutter turns overnight to the sweeping flood of a river;
living amongst the gum trees under the grey-blue of mountain
ranges, they snatched a hazardous livelihood as best they could.
Some were desperate men, like the notorious escaped convict
Donohue who 'worked' the Sydney district, or the band led by
a man named Sullivan which terrorised the area round Bathurst
in 1826. Only four years after Sullivan's era the Troopers in

Jumbo, the Downs Ranger's horse at Eastbourne, with a 'beat' around Beachy Head

One of Kingston upon Hull's four horses

The Royal Canadian Mounted Police have always given 'every man a square deal according to his deserts . . .'

Two members of the Jamaican Mounted Branch formed in 1961

this district were forced to call on the army to help deal with a party of assigned convict servants who had made an organised break from a farm at Evernden. In the ensuing years there were many savage tussles and conflicts between the Troopers and bush-rangers such as these; the police rode about their duty with their lives, literally, in their hands.

In 1833 a law providing for the appointment of two or more police magistrates for the 'Town and Port of Sydney', men empowered to enrol individuals suitable for a police force, led to the replacement of military rule by civil tribunals. Governor Brisbane's mounted policemen ceased to be under entirely military jurisdiction, and all persons arrested by the police were tried by the magistrates; five years later the Border Police Act was passed, designed to regulate the police in other towns and areas in the colony. By this time the Trooper Police in New South Wales had increased to nine officers, all magistrates by virtue of their commissions, a sergeant-major, and 156 non-commissioned officers and men. It was essential that these men representing law and order should themselves be amenable to discipline, in addition to being good shots and riders knowing something of bush craft. The best source of men fulfilling these requirements was still the army, and the majority of at any rate the rank and file were ex-soldiers—until 1860 when mounted police were first recruited from selected civilians.

The force, under a commandant, had its headquarters at Sydney, with posts of varying strength at Bathurst and other strategic points. Inevitably as New South Wales developed so did the incidence of crime. Cattle and horse thieves became more prevalent, and the recently constructed main highways, in particular the Great Western, Southern and Northern Roads, were patrolled by the Trooper Police, usually working in pairs. In addition to watching for cattle thieves, the Troopers were expected to question any other suspicious characters, and to act as escorts both to travellers and to valuable goods. Patrolling these highways was often in fact their most exciting and dangerous duty.

These Troopers were tough, dedicated men, and rode big

tough horses, capable of enduring long journeys in preference
to producing any great turn of speed. The animals were much
larger than the Australian police horses of today, none of them
being under seventeen or eighteen hands. An advertisement of
1845 required 'Two horses for the Mounted Police, not less than
four years old, and fit to carry eighteen stone'—some indication
of the total load of rider and equipment with which these horses
normally coped. Their saddles were of the old military type,
furnished with horns and with holsters for the cumbersome horse-
pistols of the time. The rider's valise was strapped behind the
saddle, his rolled-up cloak in front; when riding out on bush
duty, the horse, on whose mobility the rider's life depended, also
carried a saddle-bag containing a most necessary shoeing outfit.

During the years that New South Wales was struggling to
build up an effective police force, other states in Australia were of
course attempting to do the same. Tasmania, technically part of
New South Wales until 1825, was first colonised as Van Diemen's
Land in 1803 and continued to receive convicts for another
forty-nine years. In 1819 the settlement finally appointed police
superintendents, to take over from a type of militarily enforced
law which had included a curfew. A mounted police branch
was first formed nearly twenty years later, a curiously unbalanced
force of one aide-de-camp, one sergeant and one corporal, all in
command of five privates! Despite the fact that this small branch
provided the nucleus for the entire police force operating in Tasmania today, this is the only State so far to have done away with
all its police horses—a policy that the public appear to regret,
since twice recently, within the span of five years, the mounted
police of Victoria have been imported to add colour and his-
torical interest to the annual Agricultural Show at Hobart.

The history of the police of the outlying settlements which
later became Victoria began in 1836, when three policemen, dis-
missed for drunkenness from the force in New South Wales, were
sent to Melbourne, or Port Philip as it was then called. Two of
these exponents of law and order were speedily discharged from
their new post for the same offence, but later two separate bodies

of police were started from the small reinforcements still supplied by New South Wales. One detachment was set up in Melbourne, close to the present-day police station at Bourke Street West, the other deployed at Geelong to deal with recalcitrant aborigines—the black inhabitants of Australia since time immemorial, whose lands were being invaded by the settlers, often with unknowing desecration of places sacred to aboriginal ancestor-worship. Although not a separate mounted unit, many of these first police in Victoria, as in other areas, rode horses because of the immense distances involved, and because the horse was the accepted mode of travel. The first depot for policemen and horses was at Richmond Paddock, Melbourne, the Yarra Park of today. In 1840 thirty-seven officers and men were based here, with one farrier, one servant and a Trooper's wife, employed presumably for cooking and washing.

In England in 1805 a member of the regular Bow Street Horse Patrol had been paid 5s a night, or 28s per week, and £5,000 was set aside annually to maintain the fifty or so men and horses. Thirty-five years later, the lieutenant in command of the mounted police force in Melbourne was receiving a remuneration of 6s per day, and the annual feeding of his thirty-seven officers and troopers cost £1,049 7s 6d. Obviously the unit supported the horseman's adage 'put one's horse before oneself', because its twenty-nine horses ate £2,117-worth of hay and oats per year!

At some stage in their history many Australian states employed a complement of trained aboriginal mounted police, principally to assist in dealing with marauding members of their own nationality. These units were quite separate from the black trackers whose incredible powers of following a trail had proved invaluable to the white Troopers from as early as 1826. A native force of mounted police was formed in Queensland in 1848, to protect free settlers from hostile aborigines, and remained more or less intact until it was finally dissolved at the beginning of this century. In Victoria the first, short-lived native unit was evolved in 1839, but another corps at Naree Warren was increased to twenty-four men nine years later. This force was alleged to be more noise-productive than work-conscious, and received a certain amount of ridicule. It was however employed in two of the State goldfields and also during a search for a couple of shipwrecked white women, supposed to have been captured and carried off to live with an aboriginal tribe. Not many years late these native police faded out, by which time a regular body of Trooper Police had been established.

History is vague about the first police forces in Western Australia, but by 1868 there is a record of mounted police who carried out their exacting and hazardous duties for the princely sum of £80 to £90 per year, working a seven-day week; no leave was granted to this force until 1910. In the enormous areas of South Australia policemen were mounted from the start, as they were in Northern Territory—which had the most trouble of all the States in initiating a police force, chiefly because of the sharp rises and falls in population. In this federal territory the first police station was at Palmerston and the force was used to protect the workers on the overland telegraph line between that city and Port Augusta, and to keep the aborigines in order generally. As late as 1911 Northern Territory was still having difficulty with its police force; the men were for many years sent from South Australia, and returned home after serving their regulation five years. The Territory eventually felt compelled to form its own police force, one that of necessity has always contained mounted sections.

In the course of their duty in Northern Territory the mounted police from South Australia covered the unimaginable area of 526,620 square miles, much of it on horseback but some with camels. A Camel Corps was part of the South Australia Mounted Branch for some years. As in Jordan, camels were found considerably more effective than horses on part of the rough arid terrain in the north, as well as on the Stony Desert in the south. Right up to the last years of the second world war, it was a common event in the far interior of South Australia to meet a policeman riding a camel.

When, around 1840, the Mounted Branch in South Australia first became a separate unit from the Metropolitan and Port Police, it was put under the command of a very able ex-soldier-of-fortune who had formerly led a distinctly chequered career. Under his leadership these men and their horses, as in the other Australian States, helped materially to open up new territory as well as to guard the settlers who came there. Since there was no military unit stationed in the State at that time, the mounted police acted in military as well as civilian matters, and led such colourful if dangerous lives that men of title and letters, including aristocratic foreigners, were attracted to their ranks. Their most hazardous and successful task was the safe escorting of £2,000,000 worth of gold from Victoria to Adelaide.

The first veins of quartz, gleaming with yellow gold, were laid bare in New South Wales and Victoria in the early 1850s, and a special enlarged corps of Gold Police was recruited from the original Mounted Branch for service in the goldfields. This force gave loyal service, despite the temptations attached to such work and the daily pittance the men received of 3s 3d plus provisions, with an extra 6d for sergeants. The scope of their work expanded to include supervising the mining camps and enforcing Government regulations. The miners and their claims were scattered over several hundreds of miles, which made the overall police work easier than if they had been more concentrated, but gave the men and horses long and arduous distances to cover. The Gold Police were eventually absorbed into the Sydney mounted patrols.

Compared with what happened in other parts of the world, the gold rush in New South Wales was a relatively law-abiding affair, although the smaller state of Victoria with its richer goldfields faced a more difficult situation. One sizeable disturbance occurred, on the goldfield at Ballarat : three or four hundred armed diggers, irritated by frustrated hopes of quick wealth and a tactless police hunt for unlicensed operators, entrenched themselves behind what later became famous as the Eureka Stockade, refusing to pay their licence fees and burning their licences. A detachment of mounted police and troops stormed the stockade, thirty people were killed and the revolt quashed. Apart from this incident the actual digging for gold remained orderly, and because the miners were of all types and stations, the gold rush provided some sort of lesson in democracy; it also brought a better life to the wheat farmers and owners of sheep stations, who sold their produce to the increased population.

But the finding of gold brought an unfortunate by-product, an incitement to lawlessness among the new type of bushrangers —men who unlike the old deported convicts, or ex-convicts, were in the majority Australian-born and bred, who had nothing to learn about survival in the rough bush country that harboured them, and who were after richer game than cattle. For nearly twenty turbulent years the history of the mounted police was one of sporadic warfare against violence and murder, highway robbery and the 'stick-ups' of banks in towns and of gold in transit. The lives of the courageous men and horses who sought to enforce law and order and to protect the citizens of this vast land, were always in danger, and in one period of eighteen years thirty-five Trooper policemen were killed or wounded.

In 1862 the Sydney police and the mounted patrols were merged, with a total of about 800 foot and mounted men, and the real development of the force began from this date. The Troopers now wore blue jumpers and overalls, grey pants, Napoleon boots, and waterproof capes and cloaks of military type. Except that leather leggings were *de rigeur*, there were no hard and fast rules governing the Troopers' dress on bush service. They went better armed, their old muzzle-loading carbines replaced by Terry rifles, their cumbrous horse-pistols by colt revolvers. Yet the police force was still undermanned and comparatively poorly equipped. Recruiting of the right type of man was difficult, partly owing to the lure of better rewards in the gold-fields, partly because a policeman had small social status. In addition, the Mounted Branch had trouble in obtaining enough horses equal to enduring the strains imposed on them by the long and onerous bush patrols. Inevitably the police were subject to public criticism, particularly when wanted criminals remained uncaptured, but the force fought its way through the severe test of the great bushranging outbreak to eventual public recognition and appreciation.

Over a period of time the Troopers captured many notorious criminals. Their successes grew as a new system ensured that the mounted patrols rode about the colony at irregular intervals. If no station knew when to expect a visit, it was less easy to harbour a wanted man. And as the Troopers and their horses went on their way about the bush, they made it their business to take note of those they met, and to question any suspicious characters. They rounded up and checked the activities of the gangs of horse planters and cattle duffers, who altered the brands on stolen cattle, and by 1874 bushranging in New South Wales was virtually suppressed; only a few quickly dealt with sporadic outbreaks occurred after this date. In 1900 the Troopers tracked down and arrested some aborigines responsible for a number of particularly atrocious murders in the Dubbo District, but by and large the era of lawlessness in this area had gone. The interest in bushranging shifted to the State of Victoria and the depredations of the notorious bushranger Ned Kelly, finally captured by the Victoria Trooper Police. In later years this man was made out to be something of a hero, but the newspaper reports of the times, presumably reflecting the views of their readers, put him in a very different light.

By 1911 there were 718 Trooper Policemen and 66 attached native trackers in New South Wales, some based on Sydney, the remainder distributed throughout nine country districts. By now the policing of the outlying districts was well in hand, the status of a mounted constable had risen comfortably high, and there was no lack of first-class applicants to the force. Obviously the best type of recruit was, and still is, country-bred, a man who has grown up with a knowledge of cattle and sheep and possibly ridden a horse before he learned to walk; one who knows that

> Stringy bark will light your fire,
> Green hide will never fail yer,
> Stringy bark and green hide
> Are the mainstay of Australia.

Men of urban background were also considered, of course, and a high standard was, and is, required. The Troopers not only had to be policemen, keepers of the peace, knowing how to take fingerprints and versed in all police duties, rules and Acts relating to offences, but in country districts often everything else as well— from the Registrar of a small-debts court to the issuer of birth, death or marriage certificates. 'Out back' the mounted police- man was, and in some parts still is, clerk of the petty sessions and always an indispensable help to the local magistrate; his knowledge of ambulance and first-aid work might any time be needed; and, incidentally, he has to be able to swim. All over Australia the mounted constable had become the valued and essential friend and guardian of the settlers in his district. His visits would be keenly looked for by some squatter living out back with his merino sheep, kelpie dog and horse for company; or by the wife of a drover, absent for weeks together, as she coped alone with the children, dammed the creek in an unexpected downpour, watched the dog dig out a wombat and tackled with a stick the black snake lurking under the woodpile.

The horses supplied to these New South Wales Troopers were by then of a very high standard, bred within the State, and com- paring favourably with any in Australia. Man and horse were vital to each other's life and well-being, and the Troopers were trained in veterinary work as well as in the skills of a farrier.

Although, paradoxically enough, the majority of Australia's police horses have become urbanised, most States still have them. At the Bourke Street Mounted Police depot in Sydney a regular troop of twenty-six trained men, a mounted drill instructor and assistant and six probationary constables, with their horses, oc- cupy four acres with drill ground, armoury, stables and manège. The trainees do two months of traffic duty on foot before at- tempting similar work on horseback, and as fully fledged mounted policemen serve in the section for five years.

The thirty-four horses at the depot are all bay geldings with black points, fifteen and a half hands high, with intelligent heads and good tail-carriage—a very different type from the big, heavy horses ridden by the first Trooper Police. They are mostly bought as unbroken three to five year olds from approved breeders within the State, but at this time there are three ex-racehorses with the Troop. Like some of those belonging to the London Metropolitan Police, these thoroughbreds have been presented by their owners and, again, despite their blood and racing past they give an excellent account of themselves.

The young horses are all first handled and broken-in at the police stables. The education of the majority of police horses today follows much the same lines, the overall objective being a calm, obedient animal that, because its training has not been hustled, has had plenty of time to develop its physical and mental powers. The New South Wales Police give their horses much the same schooling as that given to the young remounts at the Metropolitan training establishment at Imber Court in England, but although their schedule too can be varied to cater for individuals, the training programme is geared for an average of nine months, against the six to seven months average in England. It is claimed that none of the horses schooled at Bourke Street police stables has ever been known to buck—a proud boast, and one that probably no one would cap on behalf of Imber Court—unless of course the Australian and British interpretations of bucking are on a different level!

Very early in his training a young Sydney police horse is taken out into the thick of the city traffic, hemmed in by an older horse on either side, with three more in front and three behind to give security and confidence. He is ridden to Centennial Park, a mile from the training centre, to take part in selection drill with the older animals. Later in his training the young horse goes out with only one 'schoolmaster' escort to get accustomed to traffic around the wharves and railway stations, and anywhere he may be working in the future—good training when he may eventually be one of the twenty-four police horses in Sydney that are ridden out daily to control pedestrian crossings near schools, and in the city and suburbs during peak hours, or to take on regular traffic duty in the centre of busy street intersections. So much for the English critics of the twenties who complained that police horses in London were more hindrance than help in controlling traffic.

The 'nuisance' training is also much like that given at Imber Court, and a Sydney police horse's first introduction to the racket and atmosphere of a real-life crowd is usually on race duty at Randwick racecourse, the main track in Sydney, where it has the safety of grass under its feet should it begin to 'play up'. Unlike London police horses which have studs screwed into their shoes, or those of New York which wear rubber shoes or pads, the Australian horses do not wear any kind of anti-slipping device.

During the year the mounted police in Sydney have approximately fifty ceremonial parades. The bay horses lead processions in the city, attend State and police funerals, and provide escorts for the State Governor and the Governor General, and for the opening of Parliament. Because the Australian army no longer has mounted troops, the mounted police have also attended many distinguished visitors, including the Queen. These well-bred, well-schooled bays, ridden by the New South Wales Troopers in parade dress with white helmets, white buckskin crossbelts and gloves, and carrying the lances presented to them in 1957 by the High Commissioner for India, provide as smart a royal escort as any in the world. The men take pride in knowing that not only are they representatives of the first body of mounted police in all Australia, formed almost 150 years ago, but they carry on the magnificent traditions of those first police Troopers who played so large a part in Australia's development.

As late as 1963 there were still seventy-four police horses in Queensland; today they are reduced to a regular strength of nineteen, used mostly on ceremonial work, but with many horses and men living in country districts who can supplement the regulars on big occasions.

Horses remained the chief mode of transport in the far-reaching distances of South Australia up to the 1930s. Then cars gradually took over for bringing the law to the countryside; the last station in the settled areas to use police horses was Blyth, in 1947. Since the war the whole conception of the mounted police in this State has changed dramatically. A mounted cadre of one officer, two sergeants and twenty-four constables stationed at the police barracks at Thebarton was formed in 1951 to provide a trained nucleus. All police cadets for whatever branch of the service receive sixteen weeks' training in equitation, a form of education considered an excellent builder of fitness and character. The system provides a constant source of reinforcements for the cadre, as well as plenty of horsemen who can return to the unit when any large occasion calls for more than the regular strength.

The police breed their own traditional grey horses at Thebarton, and including the brood mares, foals and young stock, have about seventy-three of them in all. Men and horses are taken all over the State in horse transports, semi-trailers with accommodation for both man and beast. They too have replaced the army, horseless since 1946, in all ceremonial duties, and have the usual tasks connected with crowd control and park patrols. Carrying on the mounted police tradition of athletic displays, the cadre also travel to Victoria and New South Wales to give the same exhibitions of vaulting and horsemanship that they perform all over their own State. And in common with the other mounted forces, South Australians have come to realise that their horses are the most powerful agents they possess for making and keeping friendly relations with the public. Amongst the age-old scrub and open spaces of the outback of Western Australia, too, cars have still not ousted the police horses. There are around sixty on the regular strength, and some of them provided an escort for the Queen Mother during her visit in 1966.

A police horse with the apt title of Handcuffs was in 1965 the last of his kind to be used on a country station in Victoria. Way back in 1911 there were more than two hundred mounted-police stations throughout the State, but although these have now disappeared, police horses are still active. In Australia their role in civic life appears to have taken a reverse course to that of the police horses in England. The first little horse patrol attached to the Bow Street Runners worked on the turn-pikes on the outskirts of London, and the regular Bow Street horse patrol of 1805 guarded main roads up to twenty miles distant. It was after the Great War that the mounted men began a systematic street patrol in London and other cities, and they have only recently reverted to their original role of patrolling parts of the country-side. In Australia the horses which for years were the only means of conveying law and order to the outback are now in most States largely supplanted by motor vehicles, but they are coming into their own again in the larger urban areas where, as in other parts of the world, they can make a unique contribution.

The Victoria Mounted Police are located right in the heart of Melbourne, at stables in St Kilda Road said to be the finest in the southern hemisphere. The buildings, with room for fifty-four horses, were completed in 1915, but it was then wartime and they were first used as a hospital base. The horses did not take possession until four years later, and bed numbers still linger on the walls of the riding school.

In some ways it seems a pity that the police do not make more use of their own Australian walers, tough, honest horses admir-ably suited to patrol in the bush but less good-looking than those bred for work in the cities. With the exception of a few gift horses, often sent from the race-track, the Melbourne police again breed their own horses, animals of the stamp of a good half-bred hunter, at their stud depot at Westmeadows outside the city.

Like their British counterparts in London, the sergeant, senior constable and thirty constables who make up the depot at St Kilda Road do all the stable management and general mainten-ance themselves. At one stage a Melbourne mounted policeman could buy his own horse and lend it to the police commissioner. The animal was fed and looked after at police expense, but only its owner rode it. One elderly policeman on the point of retire-ment after twenty-nine years' service owned a beautiful old horse that he exclusively had ridden; when he left the service his horse went with him.

Australia of course has the edge on Britain when it comes to sunshine, and the police horses are able to live more open-air lives. At some stations each horse has a night box for sleeping, and a day box for grooming and eating from which he can stroll outside when not on duty and take the air. These animals also have a luxury that is practically unknown in Britain, a sand bath where they can roll to their heart's content, rid themselves of sweat acquired in the course of work, and gain that complete relaxation apparent to anyone who has ever watched a horse rolling.

Australian horse experts believe in the food value of molasses mixed in a mash, a custom with which the horses can find no fault. On some outback sheep stations the horses are turned loose at night with one, the night horse, wearing hobbles. Even with this hindrance on his legs a horse can graze a long way by the morning, and it was customary to keep a 50-gallon drum of molasses with a big hole in its side. One resounding bang on this in the morning and the hobbled horse would answer the summons just as quickly as his legs, with their appendages, would carry him.

The Melbourne section take on the same general duties performed by mounted policemen all over the world, with a few refinements of their own. The horses help to prevent people crossing the track during races at Flemington racecourse; at the annual Head of the River boat-racing on the Barwon River, Geelong mounted police are indispensable both for handling traffic on the river bridge, and in coping with the more uproarious ragging by the students. They are on duty for the motor racing at Sandown Park, Calder, and at Fishermen's Bend, and attend football matches—where the umpire must be thankful for the special mounted escort provided for his safety at the end of a game! The ceremonial duties follow the normal pattern, the shining horses and their riders in full regalia, with blue-and-white lance pendons fluttering, always a popular sight with the crowd. And the mounted police are often in demand to give equitation demonstrations at shows and functions.

Like the men and horses in Sydney, those in Melbourne control school crossings in the city, and take particular care of one for blind persons which is close by their depot. Curiously enough it is only comparatively recently that police horses in Australia have been fully utilised for the work that in Britain and so many other countries in the world is recognised as their particular forte

—crowd control. In Melbourne during the Moomba festivities the mounted police now patrol the Yarra Bank and Botanical Gardens until late at night, and have proved very successful in keeping parties of youths and other prospective trouble-makers on the move. In 1966 transistor radios were used on this patrol for the first time, and walkie-talkie sets have been carried for the past ten years. When a potentially ugly situation occurred a few years ago, with crowds on the banks of the Yarra getting out of hand during a Moomba beer orgy, it was the arrival of a big troop of mounted police that helped the CIB and foot police to get matters under control.

It was, however, in 1966 that four young Englishmen finally proved to people in Victoria and some other States who saw the scenes on television just what police horses can do with a recalcitrant crowd. The Beatles arrived in Melbourne, bringing in their train hordes of screaming teenagers throwing sense, propriety and property to the winds; the hysterical masses outside the Southern Cross Hotel were on the point of breaking through the cordons and barriers erected by the foot police, when eight mounted men by manœuvring their trained horses managed to restore some semblance of order.

It was the Dutch explorer Tasman who sighted 'a large land, uplifted high', as he hove to off Tarakohe in 1642 and regarded the beautiful stretch of tumbled hills and forested coastline now called New Zealand. According to the story he then lost three of his men in a brush with the fierce Maoris, and sailed away again. No one knows for certain when these ocean-roaming Polynesians set out in canoes from their Pacific Island home, and by design or by a caprice of the untamed winds and waters arrived on the lonely beaches of a land they first saw as a long white cloud on the horizon. Legend puts the date around 1150, and some say the islands were already inhabited when they arrived, but it was one hundred and twenty years after Tasman sailed off never to return that Captain Cook revisited the islands. In 1770 he sighted what is now called Mount Egmont in North Island; in 1840 the Union Jack was hoisted in both islands.

New Zealand has meant many things to many men; Utopia, opportunity, refuge or duty. The first immigrants, the missionaries and idealists, the traders and escaped convicts from Australia, came for one or several of these reasons. The bush due east from Auckland, behind the palms along the Coromandel coast, was first inhabited by Europeans seeking gold, in claims that were soon worked out. New Plymouth, south of Mount Egmont, had a settlement of whalers at Ngamotu Beach twenty-two years before the British flag was flown or New Zealand began to be a properly organised settlement.

A voluntary militia at first dealt with law and order, but six years later an 'ordinance for the establishment and maintenance of a constabulary force' was passed. In 1853 provincial police forces were set up, of necessity riding horses. They worked in Auckland, where the extinct volcanic island of Rangitoto rises from the blue waters of the bay; in those days it was a pastoral, tree-spaced little town instead of the city of today, sprawling over fifty miles and home to half a million people. They rode out amongst the fringes of the forests clothing the Tinakori Hills behind Wellington, where the gales roar in from Cook Strait, and where police duty apparently consisted largely of keeping the peace between 'tipsy sailors, sawyers and bush settlers'. For according to a newspaper of 1857, theft and violence were particularly rare in Wellington and Auckland, which each possessed a 'smart police force of about twenty men'. There were mounted policemen too in South Island, in Canterbury situated amongst the rivers, plains and mountains, the tussock lands that now graze 25,000 sheep.

When gold was found in the Scottish-originated Otago Province, amongst the prospectors and those seeking their fortune were many desperadoes and some escaped criminals from Australia. Crimes of violence were commonplace, and the goldfields' police had a demanding task in keeping the peace. Mounted police also escorted the shipments of gold to Dunedin.

In 1877 the provincial police forces were joined with the armed constabulary, which had two branches, a 'field force' chiefly concerned with troubles with the Maoris, and a 'police force'. Taupo,

at the head of Tapuaehururu Bay, was the base for the armed
constabulary, and of course needed horses for getting about. A
truly civil police force was created in 1886, and like the British
police has since worked unarmed.

After the first world war, as roads and communications improved and motor bicycles became available, the police horses
were gradually replaced. By the early thirties only Auckland,
Wellington and Christchurch still possessed them, and they were
used mainly for ceremonial duties. The last of the police horses
in New Zealand was retired about 1958.

Patrols of New York's
large mounted force
(above) work after dark
as well as by day

Rusty, a Boston police
horse in the 30's, possessed
Morgan blood

The Garde Républicaine de Paris

Cavalry Major Piero d'Inzeo and The Rock, the famous show-jumper belonging to Italy's Carabinieri

CHAPTER EIGHT

POLICING THE CANADIAN PLAINS

THE Royal Canadian Mounted Police still have enough horses to support a title that is famous all over the world, even if today they are used only for certain ceremonial events and to perform the celebrated Musical Ride. That colourful exhibition of good schooling and precision, with its intricate patterns of 'The Maze', 'The Dome', and 'The Shanghai Cross', and the 'Bridal Arch' in which half the Ride pass under the raised lances of the remainder, is almost as well known in Britain and the United States as around Canada.

The Ride is presented in various parts of Canada each year through the summer. During the numerous celebrations for the Centennial of Confederation in the summer of 1967, large crowds in every province except British Columbia were able to watch the scarlet-coated riders, with their militarised version of the cowboy hat, and lances adorned with red-and-white pennants; thousands remember the thirty-two highly trained black horses, wheeling and intersecting until they must await, fretting and stamping with impatience, the spine-chilling trumpet notes of 'The Charge'—a rousing call that launches them down the arena, where the thudding of their galloping hooves is accompanied by a rolling of drums.

Few could forget those sights or sounds, but even in Canada itself, how many think of the horses executing that Ride as anything more serious than eye-catching components of a pageant? How many know that the red-and-white pennants, fluttering above the Mounties' heads on the shaft behind the points of their 8ft bamboo lances, represent the stained rags that men of the 16th Lancers wrapped round to get a grip when the shafts became slippery with blood? The lances adopted from the Light Cavalry by the first North West Mounted Police to impress the Indians on a march across the plains in 1874 were of a type suited to grimmer forms of display.

Today, of course, the Mounties are highly mechanised and, under the control of the Minister of Justice, are the only federal police organisation in Canada. In addition they act as provincial police, except in Ontario and Quebec, and form the only police force in the 1,516,758 square miles of the Yukon and North West Territories. The RCMP headquarters is in Ottawa, and is divided into a number of administrations. Crime-detection laboratories are situated at Regina, Ottawa, Sackville and Vancouver, and to the vast and up-to-date organisation is added an Air Division, invaluable in the vast distances of Northern Canada, and a Marine Division with thirty-six vessels which work on the Atlantic and Pacific coasts, and on the Great Lakes and St Lawrence River.

Like most police forces, the RCMP use dogs—other than the teams of huskies which have in their time saved the transport situation for them in the northern snows. A police service dog section was started in 1935 with two German shepherds (alsatians), progressing through various other German breeds such as rottweillers and dobermann pinschers, back to the twenty 'shepherds' on active duty across Canada today—thoroughly trained animals used for tracking, pursuing criminals, searching for lost persons and as guards.

The dogs survive, but for some years the Royal Canadian Mounted Police have not used their horses for actual police duties —although until recently equitation was included in the recruits' training syllabus as a character and body builder, just as it still is for the cadets of the South Australian Police Force. Now that riding has been dropped from the Mounties' programme, only a few men showing a special aptitude with horses are posted each year to the Ride, although it remains as a permanent branch within the force.

The Musical Ride was first developed as a form of cavalry drill, brought to Canada by British cavalry regiments. A troop of the North West Mounted Police, the forbears of the Royal Canadian Mounted Police, performed a similar Ride, taught them by a former sergeant-major of the 9th Lancers, in 1876. Eleven years later, with the incentive of a newly acquired band and an indoor school for winter riding, several performances of the Ride were given under the direction of a previous adjutant of the 3rd (King's Own) Hussars. In those days the evolutions to music were used not only as a colourful public spectacle, but also as a welcome change in the stringent training demanded of the mounted men and of the then indispensable horses. Without the horses, indeed, the history of Canada itself might have been very different. Without them the small bands of the forerunners of the Mounties could not have penetrated immense distances into the unknown country inhabited by often unfriendly Indian tribes. Nor could the efficient federal structure that administers law and order in modern Canada have been founded. The public image of the Mounties has often been overlaid with garishly-coloured fiction; the truth is more interesting and more exciting.

The story of Canada began in the early years of the seventeenth century, when the famous navigator Henry Hudson discovered the great Bay which bears his name, and lost his life there, marooned by a mutinous crew. As time passed hunters from the east began to adventure westward and northward into the vast prairie-lands beyond the Great Lakes. Around half a century after Hudson's death, two Frenchmen, in contact with Indian tribes, heard tales of the great bay to the north and of the vast riches in skins and furs to be found in those regions. These two pioneers, failing to get any support for their proposed trading venture from the French inhabitants by the St Lawrence, from Boston or from France, eventually arrived in England, and persuaded the dashing Prince Rupert, royal soldier of fortune, to back them to the extent of sending vessels to prospect the shores of Hudson Bay. What the two Frenchmen saw there, and the furs they brought back to prove their words, induced the Prince in 1670 to secure from the easy-going Charles II a trading charter. This gave the governor and the few men of the 'Com-

pany of the Adventurers of England trading into Hudson Bay'
virtual control over territories which, with more licences added
later, extended from the Great Lakes to the Pacific, and from
mid-continent to the North Pole. The Hudson's Bay Company
retained its hold over Rupert's Land almost unopposed for the
next two centuries.

Between the years 1812 and 1815 Scottish immigrants arrived,
ousted from their homes in the north of Scotland by landlords
more concerned with sheep than with tenants. They came thankfully to the region of the Red River in the free expanses of
Rupert's Land, settling mainly in what is now Manitoba. Others
rode north-west to join them. When the provinces of the east
became the Dominion of Canada in 1867, the leaders in Ottawa
took little time in negotiating with the Hudson's Bay Company.
In 1869 the enormous and rich territory of the north-west, with
the exception of certain rights reserved to the Company, was
purchased by the Dominion of Canada, and the province of
Manitoba was created from part of the acquired land a year later.
West and north of this little province lay the Saskatchewan,
stretching almost a thousand miles to the Rocky Mountains and
northward to the Pole, a vast hunting and battle ground to
thousands of Indians, and otherwise sparsely inhabited by groups
of half-breed nomadic buffalo-hunters, a few scattered missions
and the Hudson's Bay Company trading posts.

There were not even trading posts in the farther plains. The
Indians had allowed trading visitors but this was not enough for
the white man; during the interim period, when the Hudson's
Bay Company had given up its charter, and before the Dominion of Canada had taken up actual as well as legal control, there
was ample opportunity for every kind of boot-legger, horse thief
and unscrupulous adventurer to profit from the situation. Worst
of all these white men brought whisky to trade with, the illicit
'fire-water' which demoralised Indians and others alike and
stirred up trouble amongst the tribes. Debauched Indians wiped
out parties of settlers on their travels north, and the constant
tales seeping through of treachery and general disorder impelled

the governor of Manitoba to send a man named Butler to report on the situation.

Butler set off in October 1870, and rode 900 miles to the Rockies, then wheeled north to Edmonton and so down the Saskatchewan River to Lake Winnipeg. On his return he reported that 'the region of the Saskatchewan is without law, order or security for life or property . . . and all civil and legal institutions are entirely unknown'. A man of vision, Butler suggested the formation of a force capable of guarding the interests of settlers yet to come, and independent of faction or party either in church or state. From their inception the Canadian Mounted Police have given 'every man a square deal according to his deserts, no matter who he was or to what colour the sun and the wind had burned his skin'.

The Canadian Government was still slow to move. It was May 1873 before a bill was duly adopted providing for a uniformed police force in the North West Territories—to be a semi-military body, yet largely dependent for discipline on the personality of its officers and the *esprit de corps* that would generate in the course of service. The command was to be divided up into troops of healthy men of good character, aged between eighteen and forty, active and able to ride a horse. They would be under the overall command of a commissioner, holding the rank of lieutenant-colonel. Enrolment still did not begin immediately. Then a party of white adventurers, lawless men toughened by service in the American Civil War, crossed from Montana into the Cypress Hills area on a trading expedition. In return for anything the Indians of an Assiniboine camp had to trade, the freebooters plied them with whisky until the red men were mad drunk, then shot them down with repeating rifles, men, women and children alike. This senseless butchery pinpointed a situation that was rapidly deteriorating; the Indian tribes, maddened with liquor from outlaw traders, fought each other whenever they met. White and half-breed buffalo-hunters only ventured westward in heavily-armed companies, and any explorer set out at risk of losing his scalp.

Communication was difficult, but news of what was happening

gradually percolated through, and Ottawa moved at last. Those officers of the North West Police force already appointed began immediate recruiting in the eastern provinces. The authorized strength was for 300 men and a sufficient number of horses, but in that autumn of 1873 three troops of fifty men each were despatched over a route from the head of Lake Superior. The trail utilised the water-stretches, providing plenty of flies, mud and the 'need to make skidways over the bogs, before men and horses reached the Red River and eventually 'Stone Fort', an old Hudson's Bay post twenty miles north of the present city of Winnipeg. Here this little force of 150 men, who had been sent to patrol and bring order into an ungoverned territory that extended for 300,000 square miles, overwintered—without their warm clothing, which had become frozen-in somewhere out on the trail. However they had little time for feeling the cold, learning foot-drill and police discipline, and receiving highly necessary riding instruction. Many of the horses were unbroken and their breaking, and the riding drills, continued each day while daylight lasted—unless the thermometer dropped to more than 36 degrees below zero.

Riding those horses, and others like them through the years, was enough to keep anyone warm : real broncos adept in the true art of bucking, to which they sometimes turned even when 'broken'. When one policeman's horse started its old tricks, he banged it over the head with his hat and spurred it in true cowboy style; after a few leaps the would-be bronc stopped dead in front of the still warm ashes of the camp fire—where the rider's cartridge belt gave way with the sudden strain and slipped over the horse's head. In the resulting enfilade, it was not only the horse who lit out for cover. Another bucking horse jack-knifed its rider sideways towards a perpendicular bank, 30ft above a river. It seemed that horse and rider must go over sideways-on but the policeman pulled it round and jumped out into space. They were seen, still together, swimming strongly for the bank, and emerged with the horse a wet and wiser animal.

In the late spring of 1874 three additional troops of police left Toronto and were entrained to a point on the international boundary south of the Manitoba section. They were met at Dufferin, a small settlement on the Red River, by their comrades who had ridden out from Fort Stone some weeks previously—and who were now well equipped to cope with their horses, pioneers of the fine horsemanship that was to become proverbial in this police force.

The horses that had come east with the new troops were nearly all of the handsome Eastern type. During the time in camp at the rendezvous, they spent the nights tied to the inner side of the wagons that formed a stockade, while the Western horses, more of the cow-pony type, were tethered on the outside. One night a terrific thunderstorm caused a stampede. According to an eye-witness, the prairie was transformed into a sea of flame, and a thunder-bolt crashed amongst the horses inside the enclosure. The terrified animals broke their tethers, overturned wagons, and scrambled over each other in their mad efforts to escape. An intrepid inspector managed to seize a passing horse and pursue the runaways fifty miles over the border, eventually helping to round them up and return them to camp twenty-four hours later.

On 8 July 1874, the entire force of the newly formed North West Mounted Police started on a 'pull-out' from Dufferin, a test for new harness and other equipment. After a successful trial they set off westwards into practically unknown territory. In front rode the mounted men, divided into six divisions of different coloured horses, dark bays, bays, dark browns, greys, blacks, light bays, and light chestnuts with the field-guns and mortars. Behind came seventy-three wagons, 114 Red River carts, an assortment of farming implements, cows and calves, and beef cattle, necessary as meat 'on the hoof' when buffalo were unobtainable. This trek had two main objectives : to show and establish the outward signs of law and order through the whole North-Western Territory, especially in the foothills of the Rockies, where the ease of escaping over the nearby international boundary line encouraged depredations; secondly to find a whisky-traders' rumoured stronghold, appropriately known as 'Fort Whoop-Up', said to lie in Blackfoot land, between the fork of the Bow and Belly

Rivers. A detachment was to go on north to Edmonton and a third to return to establish a headquarters near the Hudson's Bay post at Fort Pelly, on the Swan River.

For two months the expedition marched grimly on through wild and difficult country, fording rivers, scrambling through swamps and riding across endless prairies scorched by fire, where 'the eye dwells on vacancy . . . the silence is oppressive'. They encountered drought and a fierce heat that turned, as the year wore on, to the increasing cold of autumn nights. Oxen gave up, cattle died, horses broke down and men became ill, but 300 miles out from Dufferin the column reached La Roche Percée, on the river Souris, where camp was made for the sick men and animals. The main body pushed on, after another two months of testing trekking reaching the junction of the Bow and Belly Rivers. With dwindling provisions and reduced numbers of horses, they failed to find 'Fort Whoop-Up' and turned south, through immense herds of buffalo, for the Sweet Grass Hills near the boundary. After securing supplies and horses from Fort Benton on the Upper Missouri, the commissioner left this camp with two sections, and set out for Swan River. On arrival he found the headquarters incompleted and a shortage of hay due to prairie fires, so left only one section there and rode on for Dufferin. Four months and almost 2,000 miles after setting out, the commissioner and his men arrived back at their starting point.

In the meantime the troops at Sweet Grass Hills had left for the north-west guided by Jerry Potts, an invaluable half-Peigan plainsman who acted as interpreter, found the best feed and watering places for the horses, taught the lore of the buffalo, and helped to locate the by then deserted site of 'Fort Whoop-Up'. From this first assignment Jerry Potts was to remain as interpreter and friendly mentor to the North West Mounted Police until his death twenty-two years later. They reached the foothills of the Rockies at last, and began hastily to establish the first outpost of constitutional authority in the farthest west, before winter clamped down. In the improvised shelter of Fort MacLeod, these 150 faced complete isolation in the midst of thousands of warlike and drink-sodden Indians, as well as tough gangs of whisky-pedlars and horse-thieves; Canadian authority had not yet reached out to replace an administration taken over from the Hudson Bay's Company four years previously.

Weather conditions were becoming so bad for the horses that the colonel in charge sent the weakest animals, and many of the cattle, 200 miles south to Sun River. Thought for the horses took precedence, and when 'a severe snowstorm, with high wind and extreme cold, the thermometer going to ten degrees below zero' hit Fort MacLeod on 1 November, the colonel had all the remaining horses driven into the shelter of the nearby woods, 'every one blanketed and fed with oats and corn'. He was 'extremely anxious about them, and glad they got through so well'.

All through the history of the Canadian Mounties runs this thread of the attachment between men and horses. Over long, dangerous and lonely trails, in storm and blizzard, the lives of these policemen depended on their animals' endurance. One spring at the beginning of this century, the body of a young constable was found after the melting of the winter snows, a pathetic note beside him : 'Lost. Horse dead. Am trying to push ahead. Have done my best.'

Despite the difficulties of building up Fort MacLeod in the shortest time, the Mounted Police never lost sight of their objectives—to bring law and authority to white men and Red Indians alike, and to suppress the 'fire-water' trafficking, with all its appalling consequences. It did not take the tribes long to appreciate the meaning and integrity of the men wearing the 'scarlet tunic'—the red coats that had purposely been retained by the new police force, because the Indians remembered the fair-dealing they had received from British soldiers wearing the same colour. Native chiefs began to visit the police outpost, dignified red men of the Crees, Assinimoines and Salteaux, as well as those of the Blackfeet Confederacy. When Crowfoot, the great Okimaw of the Blackfoot, rode into camp to shake hands and smoke the Pipe of Peace with the commanding officer, it was a turning point in the history of the Mounties. Courage and loss of life was called for, but the police motto *Maintiens le Droit*—

Uphold the Right—gradually became a recognised maxim on the plains. 'Before you came,' said one chief, 'the Indian had to creep along, not knowing what would attack him, but now he is not afraid to walk erect.'

Meanwhile, on 27 October 1874, the small detachment left at La Roche Percée set out on a nightmare march to temporary winter quarters at the Hudson Bay post at Edmonton, 850 miles away. They rode by way of Fort Ellice and Carlton, with horses that were already played-out. Both water and pasture proved scarce, for 500 miles they had no grain, and as the nights got colder the troopers had to lift many of the horses on to their legs in the mornings, and rub their stiffened joints before they could get going. The animals were so weak during the last twenty-five miles that they could scarcely move over the hard-frozen ground, but they reached Edmonton at last, to receive the friendly help that was always offered between the men of the company and the new police taking over their responsibilities.

Before long co-operation between police and Indians was to be well tested. In return for help across the border in fighting the United States cavalry, the Sioux, the most powerful tribe of American Indians in the north-western states, offered the Canadian Blackfoot booty and, afterwards, aid in wiping out the mounted police and settlers in their territory. When this offer was rejected the Sioux then threatened their hoped-for allies, and the police promised the Blackfoot that if necessary they would fight to protect Chief Crowfoot's realm.

Since 1862 there had been almost incessant hostilities between the Sioux and the United States Army. When, fourteen years later, gold found near Dakota brought white prospectors rushing from the east, the invasion, coupled with disregarded treaties, spurred the Indians to action. Led by Sitting Bull, the Sioux made a stand and completely wiped out five troops of the 7th US Cavalry under General Custer; they then escaped retribution over the international boundary into Canada. Here Sitting Bull promised to obey the Queen's laws, but the presence of this warlike chief and the 5,600 members of his tribe was a deterrent to would-be settlers and a constant source of anxiety to the 214 mounted police, responsible for the security of life and property along the hundreds of miles of boundary. There was always the risk that Canadian tribes might join the American Indians and rise against the settlers and police, and the Sioux had to be kept from the already depleted buffalo hunting-grounds of the Blackfoot. Fortunately Crowfoot and his Blackfoot warriors remained loyal, and five years later the combined efforts of the mounted police and a sagacious French-Canadian trader prevailed on Sitting Bull to accept an offer of peace and a reserve in the United States, and he and his tribe returned over the border.

From 1873 onwards the whole settlement of the West went on under the guidance of the mounted police, responsible for the administration of the laws of the Dominion from Manitoba to the Rockies. There was plenty of diversity of duty. The Mounties dealt with victims of winter blizzards and starvation, attended to weddings, funerals, accidents and illnesses, battled against prairie fires and smugglers, and trailed and apprehended gamblers, horse and cattle thieves and murderers. As the settlements spread there were mining and lumber camps to oversee, and the development of new villages and towns called for the enforcement of law and order. The ten-year building of a railway linking east and west brought special problems: the Indians resented an invasion of their territory by 4,000 railway labourers, and order had to be kept during strikes.

In 1877 the Blackfeet Confederacy signed a treaty giving the Dominion full sovereignty in the Canadian West. Gradually the Indians were moved to reservations away from the boundary, but it was not easy for them. Their means of livelihood, the free, unfettered existence of buffalo hunting, was replaced with the restrictions of territory and law imposed by white men. At times there was famine in the camps, to fan the unrest shown by half-breeds on the Saskatchewan and growing amongst the Crees and Assiniboines in the north. Early in the summer of 1884 the police had warnings of unrest amongst half-breeds in the Battleford area. Later the appearance of Louis Riel, a half-breed trouble-maker, the originator of past disturbances around the Red River, intensified a dangerous situation. By March 1885 rebellion was inevitable, many of the Indians joining the half-breeds. The northern detachments of police had to be reinforced, and the commissioner set out from Regina with ninety officers and men and sixty-six horses, on a forced march in bitter weather. The column reached Prince Albert, an outpost of Battleford, after slipping past the insurgent guards, and pressed on to Fort Carlton, but already there had been a clash. Fifty-three mounted police aided by forty-one civilian volunteers from Prince Albert had taken on nearly 400 half-breeds and Indians at Duck Lake, and had been thrown back with casualties. This was the signal and rebellion flared.

In the reserve up near the Hudson's Bay post of Fort Pitt, Big Bear and his Cree Indians massacred nine whites, and the mounted police lost a constable while holding the post with a handful of men. At Battleford the events at Duck Lake stirred up another powerful Cree element under Chief Poundmaker. Here a mounted police inspector organised a home-guard with his few men, for the safety of 400 white women and children, barricaded behind a stockade for many weeks. And when all the wires were cut, a young constable rode out alone and was pursued for sixty miles as he carried a dispatch to Swift Current. All Canada was aroused by news of the rebellion, a call to arms was made, and for three months regiments from both east and west aided the mounted police. Fortunately the Blackfoot once more remained loyal, and the troubles ceased with the defeat of the rebels on 16 May 1885.

After the rebellion the North West Mounted Police were increased to a strength of 1,000 rank and file, a number of Indians and half-breeds were attached as trailers and scouts, and the force was distributed more widely over the plains.

During the next few years the West changed rapidly. Immigration and new settlements increased, wheat farming supplemented the cattle, and many Indians, under government instruction and encouraged by those mounted policemen able to see what the area needed, learned farming and ranching—even if some of the younger braves still preferred to rustle their cattle and horses, rather than raise them. The mounted police had to heal the difficulties left over from the rebellion, and began a system of regular patrols. By 1894 the force had been so successful in reassuming control in the West that its strength was gradually reduced by 200.

Within a short time a stampede to the Yukon goldfields, with the lawlessness that always follows a gold rush, presented new and urgent problems, and sent a small selected force of Mounties to establish the most northerly police outpost in the British Empire. A year later 266 officers and men were stationed in this region, and when the Yukon became a separate territory, its population around 20,000, the police were supplemented for a while by a special force of 200 Canadian soldiers.

Meanwhile the detachments in the plains were still showing the initiative that gave them their reputation for 'always getting their man'. One constable in pursuit of an escaped criminal found that the Saskatoon ferry was out of order, his way barred by the river. Not to be deterred, he commandeered a railway hand-car, persuaded his incredulous horse to climb on to it, and worked his way across the trestle railway bridge over the foaming water many feet below. History does not reveal which was the most astonished, the constable's horse or the convict; the latter was outwitted by the manoeuvre, and overtaken and arrested just as he was filing off his leg-iron.

After the South African war—in which over 200 mounted policemen served—300,000 people began to stream westwards, to territory that had become tenable now law and order was preserved. The mounted police expanded until by 1904 there were eight divisions, with eighty-four detachments. In that same year the force received the prefix 'Royal', bestowed by King Edward VII in recognition of its magnificent record of service. Seven years later the red coats and quality horses of the Royal North West Mounted Police were to be seen in London, at the coronation of King George V.

It was not the first time this force from Canada had visited London to enhance a royal occasion. On 22 and 23 April 1897, a detachment was inspected at Fort MacLeod prior to sailing to England as part of the military contingent from Canada attending the celebration of Queen Victoria's Diamond Jubilee. By 28 April the men and horses were assembled at Regina, where they trained for the next few weeks; by the end of May the horses, sent by rail to Montreal, had sailed for England. Then trouble broke out once more at Duck Lake and it seemed as though the men would be delayed in following their animals. Some of them were sent off to help catch an Indian called Almighty Voice, wanted for cattle stealing and gaol breaking. Two were killed when the Indian resisted arrest, and Almighty Voice himself and two other Indians were shot during the fracas. By 1 June the others were in Winnipeg, three days later in Quebec and on the 15th the superintendent, Bowen Parry, and his contingent disembarked at Liverpool.

England was not entirely an unknown quantity to the super-intendent. As a young man he had graduated, first class, at the Royal Military College in Kingston, Ontario, and was then as-signed to a British Guards Regiment. Turned down on medical grounds he returned to Canada, aged nineteen, with no prospects and only military training. When the North West Mounted Police began recruiting for the Riel Rebellion, he enlisted in the force. A resourceful, quick-thinking man of action, largely instrumental in the defeat of Big Bear and his Cree Indians after the massacre at Fort Pitt, Parry took charge at Prince Albert when the rebellion was over, and quickly rose in both rank and responsibilities. Through the years he and his men trailed and brought to justice numbers of cattle-killers, mail-robbers and other malefactors, but he was much concerned with the future of the half-breeds and Indians as well as with the thousands of settlers by then pouring into the west. Eventually he rose to the rank of General, and as Commissioner of the North West Mounted Police held the longest term of service in the supreme command.

When they arrived in London the Canadian contingent were quartered at Chelsea Barracks and quickly rejoined their horses. Two of the animals had died at sea, and one from pneumonia since landing, but the remainder were fit and, strangely, seemed to take no exception to London streets after Canadian prairies.

Their riders had the excitement of attending Ascot races, where they saw Persimmon, the Prince of Wales's legendary horse, win the Gold Cup. Superintendent Parry 'much admired the beauty of the dresses and the lovely scenery' there, but had trouble with his men over their own dress—for some reason 'duck' being preferred to their scarlet full uniform.

On the remaining days before the Jubilee, the Canadians marched to Victoria Embankment to learn their parade positions, and into the East End. They rode through the City down Whitechapel to Victoria Park and, being the Rear Guard, unhappily arrived too late for lunch. After a glass of beer they rode back to barracks in company with thousands of Imperial Troops, and through 'immense crowds who were most good-natured and cheered incessantly'.

The great day dawned and the Canadian contingent formed the Rear Guard of the Colonial Procession at St Paul's, drawn up on the north side of the opening to Cannon Street. Although it was a 'beautiful day and a wondrous sight' and the Queen 'looked all over the Police very carefully as she passed', the superintendent seemed more impressed by the sound of the 'Old Hundredth' sung in the subsequent service at St Paul's, when 'it was taken up in succession by the different streets, and as it rolled down the vast throng and growing more and more faint it was awe-inspiring indeed'.

On 22 June the contingent rode to Hyde Park for a Review. Although, sadly, it was the Australians who were complimented by the commander-in-chief on having adopted 'a serviceable uniform', the Canadians made a gallant sight. And they were certainly not guilty of the slight faux-pas committed by a section of the Royal Canadian Mounted Police thirty-seven years later—when, uncertain of the whereabouts of the Mansion House, the 'scarlet-coated riders from the great spaces of the Dominion' rode, with eyes rigidly to the front, straight by a bewildered Lord Mayor waiting to take the salute from the balcony above. Nor was any horse guilty of behaving like the one which, when the Mounties rode through the city en route for the International Horse Show at Olympia in the thirties deposited his rider in the road, to be succoured by Colonel Laurie of the Metropolitan Mounted Police.

The Canadian contingent were reviewed twice more by the Queen, once at Aldershot, and again at Windsor where they were quartered with the Blues, and where Superintendent Parry was presented. At a ceremony in Buckingham Palace Gardens the Prince of Wales presented medals, but he was apparently uncommunicative: all he said was 'Curious way of carrying ammunition'—referring to the Mounted Police waist-belts, with cartridges held in loops. Two days later the Canadian police horses were handed over to the British Army, and the contingent sailed for home, leaving their superintendent to visit Salisbury Plain to study cavalry methods with the Royal Scots Greys.

To Canadian eyes the officers' horses appeared very good, but those of the troopers 'coarse looking', some 'very unsightly', and overall broader and heavier than the accustomed Western animals. The superintendent was privately informed that some British regiments were disgracefully horsed, but that the Scots Greys possessed the best animals. On the whole he considered they were better horsed than the North West Mounted Police, and found their saddles comfortable. He was intrigued by the way the chargers were tethered, fore and aft, with a heel rope much like that used by the Teheran Mounted Police today, and noted the lack of lung disease and contracted feet. He was impressed by all the mounted drill, but watching the cavalry dismounted for carbine work convinced him that his police 'are much better trained on foot'.

Possibly the young Canadian preferred the horses to their riders. After three days he was not able to say that he felt any more at home, and though he was lent a pony to visit Stonehenge, he rode there by himself, 'feeling it somewhat . . . quite out of all their arrangements'. However his visit taught him three lessons: to train his police horses more carefully, to buy a stronger horse, to adopt a new saddle; and on leaving he found 'all the officers of the Greys most kind in their parting wishes', pressing him to visit them again. He in turn, 'found them on acquaintance most delightful men'.

Men and horses of the Carabinieri have civilian as well as military duties

The strong, big horses ridden by the Stuttgart Mounted Police are dressage schooled

The Great War came and went with all its attendant tragedies, and although the Mounties were not released for overseas service until 1918, the demands on the force were then so heavy that their home strength fell to about that of the original in 1874. The Government then put the North West Mounted Police upon a new and permanent establishment, and they were assigned the duty of enforcing Dominion legislation everywhere west of Port Arthur and Fort William. Two years later the force absorbed the Dominion Police, a federal organisation, and became the Royal Canadian Mounted Police.

Horses were still used between the two world wars, but the police gradually became more mechanised. Soon after the outbreak of war in 1939, the Mounties supplied the First Provost Company for the Department of National Defence, which was almost immediately sent overseas.

Up to 1940, and in the days when the horses were still used for recruit training, the mounted police obtained their remounts from outside sources. From that year they began to breed their own. The site selected was near the Assiniboine Camp, where the inhabitants were shot down by white freebooters in 1873; Fort Walsh was built by the North West Mounted Police two years after the massacre, being from 1878 until 1882 the headquarters of the force. The 15,360 acres of the ranch lie in a valley, almost 5,000 ft above sea level, and here two thoroughbred stallions, Faux Pas, a winner of the Ascot Gold Vase, and Williegeorge, a leading Canadian sire, run with half-bred mares. The object today is to produce quality black horses of from 15.3 to 16.2 hands, suitable to fill the ranks of the Musical Ride, and to uphold the force's high standards when on ceremonial parade. Possibly some of those Royal Canadian Mounted Policemen reported in the papers of May 1967 as having to link arms as they struggled to hold back a demonstrating crowd felt a passing regret for the few solid, well-mannered animals that could have done the job in their stead.

CHAPTER NINE

AROUND THE WORLD

ON 2 June 1953, the Prime Minister of Northern Ireland took part in the Queen's Coronation Procession. He was attended by two members of the Royal Ulster Constabulary on horseback, and since even in those days there was no mounted section in this police force, the marshalling of equine equipment and accoutrements held over from the Royal Irish Constabulary era presented considerable difficulties. On the day, however, the horses paraded correct in saddlery and trappings that would have been familiar to that superintendent of the Canadian North West Mounted Police who attended Queen Victoria's Jubilee more than half a century before.

Superintendent Bowen Parry indeed paid a visit to the Royal Irish Constabulary in 1897 before his return to Canada, after leaving his friends of the Royal Scots Greys. Before setting off for Ireland he travelled to Tewkesbury, first-class by rail from Salisbury for 19s 6d, to stay with a clergyman friend. In this quiet retreat the superintendent encountered typical British weather, 'a most soaking rain', found a drenched tramp 'respectably dressed in a frock coat' drying out in the church porch, and watched that bearded giant of sport, W. G. Grace, play in a cricket match. He appears to have appreciated the beauties of the English countryside, the quiet country roads, the view from a hill when the sun had just set and the twilight faded—'such scenery is England's charm and makes me sorrowful to think I may never see it again'. Certainly he found a contrast in the slum quarters of Dublin, which 'smelt awfully' and were a 'disgrace to civilisation', but Parry fell for the magic of the Irish landscape around the Wicklow Hills. He found the men of the Royal Irish

Constabulary in Dublin 'very fine fellows', who seemed to take the keenest interest in their instruction, even if they could teach the North West Mounted Police nothing when it came to drill. Before sailing for home he attended a ceremony in Dublin Park 'where nearly all the Imperial horses in Ireland were reviewed by Lord Roberts'.

Dublin ceased to have police horses after 1917, but in the future two blood stallions from Ireland may possibly be exported as far afield as Bahrein, to add substance to the mounts of a police force rather different from the Royal Irish Constabulary. This idea may never mature, and in the meantime the Bahrein Mounted Police ride pure Arabian horses, beautiful stallions bred at the palace of the Ruler of Bahrein, Shaikh Isa Bin Salman Bin Hamad Alkhalifah.

This mounted police section is large enough to perform regular duties, and therefore unique in the Persian Gulf, where the other local 'mini-sections' do not rise above half a dozen horses in strength and are purely ceremonial in concept. The Bahrein unit was founded in the mid-1930s by an Englishman, Sir Charles Belgrave, the political adviser at the time, and has proved so successful that the original twenty horses have been increased to forty. The senior officers are British and the saddlery comes from England, but the officer in charge of the mounted section, Assistant Sub-inspector Zaid Juma, is one of the original twenty policemen, a dedicated man who has never served in any other department.

The stallions are housed in clean, roomy stabling at the Police Fort (Headquarters) just outside Manama. The general air of tidiness and discipline is impressive, and the horses are immaculately groomed and in the pink of condition. As always in these hot countries, grass is not available, and like the police horses of Iran and Jordan, those of Bahrein have alfalfa and barley, which in this case is imported, as their staple food.

The stallions are trained in crowd-control work, but so far have not been required to put their prowess in this field to the test. Many of their duties are ceremonial in some degree or

150   POLICE HORSES

another; they provide a mounted escort if the Ruler visits the
political residence or British Consulate, and a ceremonial parade
is held at the police fort itself on the third Thursday of every
month. In addition, these policemen ride regular daily patrols
through Manama town, and out to the fishing villages around the
island. The police horses perform their most useful work in these
outlying areas, which are often inaccessible even by Land Rover,
and where the sight of an elegant, fiery horse carrying the
exponent of law and order 'scares the hell' out of incipient
felons.

Bahrein is very hot indeed during the summer, and although
these Arabian horses seem able to take temperatures as high as
the mid-summer 140°F or more, for their greater comfort they
are moved to cooler quarters on the State farm at Budai from
June until September. Like most horses of Arabian blood, they
are resistant to disease, and only one has had to be destroyed
during the last five years. They are of course vaccinated against
the dreaded scourge of African horse sickness.

It was thought to be not African horse sickness but an undiag-
nosed brain infection that killed off 192 mares at the police stud
farm in South Africa during 1944. With the approval of the late
Field-Marshal Jan Smuts, the stud had been started eight years
previously at Grootdam (Large Lake), in the Kimberley district,
where the horses could have the advantages of normal rainfall
and a daily average of $9\frac{1}{2}$ hours sunshine, combined with the
short, sweet grassveld on which they thrived.

Originally the stud was largely stocked with animals from a
stud near Kimberley that was being closed by De Beers, the
amalgamated diamond-mining company. From this source the
police acquired six big blood stallions of proved endurance and
speed, 500 Percheron mares—an active draught breed, that
originated in France some hundred years back and is said to have
Oriental blood—263 geldings, 60 fillies and 270 colts. Ten years
later the number of stallions had risen to ten, including Tego,
presented to the then Minister of Justice by the Portuguese
President, and several well-known ex-racehorses such as Bally

Jamesduff, winner amongst other trophies of the Metropolitan Handicap and Short Ridge Crown Stakes.

But luck was not with the police venture, for scarcely had the stud recovered from its first epidemic than an outbreak of anthrax claimed a further 186 mares. The drought of 1945-8 then took its toll, and since it was about this time that the police began to use motor transport on a large scale they ceased to breed their own horses, and the animals were sold off at auctions. The stud was closed, but this did not mean the end of one of the oldest mounted police forces in the world.

The first guard or picket of police in the Cape was formed in 1668, and of necessity consisted of mounted men. In 1806, a year after the regular Bow Street Horse Patrol was inaugurated in London, the Cape Regiment, a semi-military police force, was begun. By 1904 there were police units in the Transvaal, Orange Free State and Natal, in addition to the newly formed Cape Mounted Police. The well-equipped South African Police Force of today was established in 1913.

Before the police bred their own horses at Grootdam, they purchased them from throughout the Republic and South West Africa, young and untrained but endowed with the qualities of their predecessors, fine animals which had been bred from Persian Arabs and from Arabian and Barb horses imported from Java in 1653. Those Cape Horses were evolved originally as riding and draught animals for the settlers; they needed exceptional endurance to cope with the great treks outwards from the Cape, pushing forward through forest and savannah, over grass-veld and Karoo scrub, and scrambling between the poorts of precipitous mountains. They became of such renown that the British army used them for cavalry chargers in India, and during the Balkan wars horses bred near the Hamtam Mountains in the Karoo took part in the Charge of the Light Brigade; during the Boer war the British 'Tommies' were so impressed with the qualities and stamina of the horses ridden by the Boer commandos that they lost no time in acquiring similar animals. There is Cape Horse blood in Australian walers, from animals landed off trading ships sailing from the Cape of Good Hope in the seventeenth century, and the Basuto Pony in South Africa is a direct descendant.

Before 1937 the young entry for the mounted police were sent by rail to the South African Police College at Pretoria. On arrival they were herded in groups of ten into a kraal known as a 'bucket', to be lassoed and haltered for the first time in their lives. The first part of their training bore little resemblance to that given at Imber Court, and in general use today. Blind-folded and saddled, these wild young horses ran free in the bucket for a while before being bridled, and were then mounted by one of the intrepid 'rough riders', who received well-earned extra pay for the privilege. There was little those horses did not try on in the way of bucking, pig-jumping and kicking, and any rough rider dislodged was merely asked the world-wide question, 'Who ordered you to dismount?' This saddle-breaking did not last for more than ten minutes a day, and care was taken to see that the horse did not develop a dislike for its rider. By the end of five days most of the horses were ready to begin their three months' course of obedience training, and were made fit for the subsequent long hours of patrol duties. Any animal still unsuitable for police work after six months was sold.

Today 173 police horses are on duty at thirty-five stations in the Transkei, Border and Natal areas. A further seventy-four are kept at the Police College in Pretoria and are used for training mounted students, ceremonial duties, and gymkhanas and jumping competitions.

Many of the horses bred at their Grootdam stud added lustre to the image of the South African Mounted Police, but perhaps Tiger was the most famous. A versatile performer with a host of achievements, the high-light of his career was when he completed the seventeen international fences of the Grand Open Championships at the Rand Easter Show without a fault—and without a saddle for the last two jumps, his rider discarding it when the girth broke. Winston was another famous horse, for many years the holder of the South African high-jump record. Turk, the last of the Grootdam horses still in work, has won dozens of prizes, and was ridden by the Queen when, as Princess Elizabeth, she paid a visit in 1947. Since that date Turk has taken part in every opening of Parliament. Selbourne, a majestic jet-black horse, led the procession at the military funeral of Field-Marshal Smuts.

If it is virtually unheard of for a foal to be born grey, it is— as previously mentioned—equally unusual for a young horse to be white. Like humans, grey horses become lighter with age, but Fleur was already white when the South African Police acquired him as a yearling in 1948. He became well-known by the thousands who watched his dignified bearing at the annual openings of Parliament from 1955 to 1962. He was on ceremonial duty when the late Hon. J. G. Strydom was elected Prime Minister, and had also to form part of the escort at his funeral. Fleur is now a pensioner, enjoying peace and quiet after long service.

Back in Norway, when the police horse Tyra was retired from duty off the broad Karl Johansgate boulevard and the other Oslo streets, she was ridden in procession with an escort of schoolchildren—young people expressing the Norwegian fondness for animals. Citizens of this northern capital are proud of their eighteen handsome police horses, and extend their admiration to the mounted police themselves. The public here are the first to acknowledge that horses can deal as efficiently with riots today, as they did during the Oslo disorders of the 1920s, when they were able to handle the situation without resorting to the military. Teenage disturbances are effectively ended by one policeman on foot with a megaphone telling the crowd to disperse, his demands backed up by two mounted policemen behind him; oddly enough one of the 'weighty arguments' that at last persuaded the Norwegian Home Office to sanction a mounted police force of sixteen horses in 1893 was that 'guttersnipes, adolescents and youngsters gathered in large crowds and conducted themselves in a scandalous way in public areas'.

All in all, however, modern Oslo is a peaceful city, and there is no need for mounted policemen such as an efficient but notoriously tough officer of the 1920s, whose very approach and name

used to quell the spirits of the unruly. Once during a riot outside
the police headquarters there came the sound of a horse's hooves
and someone yelled, 'Here comes Braekke!' The street emptied
within seconds—and round the corner at a brisk trot came a
horse-drawn cab!

The Norwegian horses are schooled in crowd control, as well as
in ceremonial duties, and the mounted officers use their 'aids' with
such discretion that—as, probably, in large cities in various parts
of the world—the uninitiated remain convinced that a police
horse, moving his rump sideways to push back a crowd and clear
the way, does so as his own bright idea. Few Norwegian-bred
horses, most of which belong to the Baltic Pony group, are of the
required type for the police, who prefer big, strong animals which
can withstand pressure, give their riders a good overhead view,
and make a suitable psychological impression on the public. Suitable horses are therefore imported from Sweden, handsome
animals of the type used by the Swedish mounted police, and of
excellent temperament.

So it is that the same type of horse patrolling the Oslo streets
is also keeping a watchful eye on the suburbs and parks that adorn
the solid architecture and revolutionary shipyards of Sweden's
biggest seaport, Gothenburg. Travellers from the Continent
arriving in Sweden via Malmo will find twenty of these same
attractive horses doing the same kind of work, and a division of
forty-seven of them is stationed for duty in Stockholm. There may
be no police horses amongst the cantons of Switzerland, nor on
the Acropolis-dominated streets of Athens—where the police
occasionally borrow military horses for riot control—but in
Sweden, for all its ultra-modern ideas, the mounted units are so
valued that the numbers of police horses have steadily increased
from the time they were first used at the end of the nineteenth
century.

The horses are ridden in snaffles, with double bridles for ceremonial occasions. The mounted officers dispensed with swords
in favour of leather whips many years ago, and when they ride
out on night patrol the officers wear white reflecting shoulder-
belts, a sensible safety measure duplicated in the reflecting plates

hanging from the stirrup irons and the white 'gaiters' or tendon boots worn by the horses.

There seems to be little consistency in the way different police forces look on a mounted section. In cities like Oslo and Stockholm, London, New York or Sydney, the police horses are used ever more frequently on traffic control as the traffic density thickens with the years; yet in Paris, it was thought that 'the presence on busy road junctions of a guardian of the peace on horseback, presented a danger as much for the horse and rider as for the motorist'.

A certain reluctance seems to have been shown by the Prefect of Police of Paris ever to start a civilian mounted section at all. The newspaper *La Liberté* mentions the existence of a gendarme on horseback in February 1848, but the force which that gentleman represented cannot have survived for long. Eight years later, and in the two following years, there is once more talk of creating 'gardes on horseback', with the object of 'maintaining the security of the citizen in the streets of Paris', as though the originals had never existed. It was 1909 before a try-out took place in the Rue de la Paix; history does not relate exactly what the police horses were required to do even then, and the results were recorded as 'non-conclusive'. They remained so for the next fourteen years. In 1922 a supplementary credit of 80,000 francs appeared in the budget of the Municipal Council of Paris, as an allowance for the purchase and keep of twelve horses provided to guarantee the 'regularity of the circulation'. Mounted police regularly controlled traffic on all the principal road junctions such as the Place de la Trinité, until the 'circulation' reached such enormous and intricate proportions that in 1937 the horses were, perforce, removed; a necessity that will be appreciated by anyone who has ever driven in Paris.

This decision only affected the civilian mounted police. There is another force which comes under the direction of the Prefect of Police, a military force which contains a regiment of cavalry vitally concerned with the supervision of the capital. The activities of the Garde Républicaine de Paris are part of the Parisians' everyday life, and the cavalry regiment is both the last mounted unit of the French army, and the last horse formation in France having any civilian duties for keeping order and security.

There are two squadrons in the cavalry of the Garde de Paris, one mounted on greys and one on bays. The majority of the 550 horses are Anglo-Normans, an excellent type of military horse with a long ancestry going back, via the Norfolk Trotter, Young Rattler, to the Godolphin Arabian. The remainder are Anglo-Arabs, with a small percentage of English thoroughbreds. The horses are bought as three-year-olds in Normandy, the Charolais and the Tarbes region. At four years old they are schooled at the Garde's centre of equestrian instruction at St-Germain-en-Laye, near Paris. As their training progresses they are schooled in dressage, and accustomed to the hazards of the Paris streets. Some of the horses take part in equestrian sports and competitions, and those showing special aptitude are trained for exhibition work. Regimental duties are undertaken, both mounted and on foot, and the horses are used for escort and ceremonies, for keeping order, particularly on the Paris racecourses, and for purposes of prestige and propaganda, both in France and abroad.

France is not the only country to possess a mounted force military in concept which performs civilian police duties. In Spain the Guardia Civil is a militarily conceived police force; when organised in 1844 by the Duke of Ahumada it consisted of nine companies of cavalry. In those first days the horses, tack, uniforms and equipment belonged to the *guardias* themselves, bought with money advanced by the State and gradually deducted from their pay. Once the divisions were formed, each *guardia* had to bring with him a horse which conformed with the required standards. When his term of service came to an end, he could either trade in these belongings or take horse and all into 'Civvy Street'.

This custom led to great financial hardship, particularly if a horse became ill or had an accident, and the Government was forced to provide funds for buying the horses. This scheme did not work either, and in 1845 led to the forming of a Horses' Insurance Association, followed three years later by a fund for replacing horses, which enabled each man gradually to be repaid the value of his animal.

Various other ideas were tried between the years 1857 and 1893, when a Buying and Training Centre was set up at Getafe (Madrid), working in conjunction with the army. Unbroken young horses were obtained from the same sources as those for the army, and two-year-old colts destined for the Guardia Civil were bought and run out at the centre under the best possible conditions. This proved an economical method of gaining the best animals for the force, but it was impossible to cope with the required numbers and many *guardias* were left horseless in consequence. The centre was closed in 1899, and a Cavalry Supply Commission began to buy direct from horse-dealers. For a while this method once again ensured the best horses being obtained, but then once again the scheme failed through lack of funds and a consequent lowering in quality. In 1905 the Commission was dissolved and incorporated into the General Army Command, and after 1906 the cavalry regiments and most of the army regiments were supplied with horses by the Guardia Civil. By the early 1940s the process had been reversed. The Cavalry and Veterinary Headquarters was set up within the administration of the Guardia Civil to deal with everything to do with horses, mules and police dogs. When it came to buying for the Guardia Civil, its own veterinary officer and the chief commandant of training services sat in on the committee.

In 1847 the Guardia Civil possessed 1,535 horses. Today it has nearly 7,000.

Even in this day and age there are several other mounted police forces which have increased their numbers with the years. At the time when St Paul is said to have been ship-wrecked in a bay on the islands of Malta, the Melita of the New Testament, there were probably no horses there of any kind, but in about 1530, when the island was part of the Holy Roman Empire, the Emperor Charles V gave Malta to the Knights of St John of Jerusalem in 'perpetual sovereignty.' These champions of Christianity had been driven from Palestine and from the Island of Rhodes by the Turkish Sultan Soliman, and being horsemen would scarcely have arrived in their new home without at least some of their mounts. Certainly there were horses on the island prior to 1813 when, in the same year as the Treaty of Paris made the Maltese British subjects, the Malta Police Force in its present form was born and enlisted the aid of an existing group of horsemen known as Dragoons, to help maintain law and order. The exact date of the formation of the present Mounted Branch is unknown, but some of the older generation still refer to its members as 'Id Draguni'.

Up to 1850 the Malta Police Force was poorly manned, its numbers mainly deployed in the capital city and principal towns, the horses patrolling the countryside and villages. At night, the sound of hooves clattering round the terraced hillsides, the lights from the policemen's lanterns flickering across a wheat field or revealing the outline of some ancient Tarxien Neolithic temple, were both reassuring to the law-abiding and a deterrent to the criminal. On one of these patrols on an April night in 1860, a police officer was shot and killed while he and his companions were investigating four suspicious characters near a farmhouse in the village of Zabbar.

Today there are thirty police horses in Malta, eighteen of them 'Irish Hunter' type geldings, and the remainder stallions, mainly of Arab stock and the kind of animal that the Knights of St John, the Hospitallers as they were called, would have brought from Palestine. All the horses are 15.3 hands or more, bays, chestnuts or greys being preferred. In common with mounted policemen the world over, the Maltese men take the greatest pride in their horses' looks and well being—care that stands them in good stead for the friendly contest at the annual horse show when they compete for a trophy for 'The Best Mounted Policeman'.

Stuttgart is one of the world's big cities which have chosen to continue using police horses. The mounted police there show off their thirty horses to an appreciative public at various civic functions. The animals are dressage schooled, and larger, tougher animals than those of Malta. Many of them are Holsteins, one of the oldest breeds in Germany, descendants of the Marsh horse of 1300, the 'Great Horse for War and Tourney' that has an infusion of oriental and Spanish blood, with a dash of the English Cleveland Bay, and is often a good show-jumper. Others are Hanoverians, strong, well-made animals of 16 to 17.1 hands from the west of Germany, and there are a few thoroughbreds bred in the State of Wuerttemberg.

This mounted police force, the 'Berittene Schutzmannschaft' as it was first called, was started in 1889 to help control the crowds and extra traffic born of special occasions, and to patrol the large areas of open country and forest where the people of Stuttgart take their leisure—duties that are much the same today, those for which, despite the usual suggestions that motor cycles and cars might be cheaper and more effective, horses have held their own.

The Stuttgart police quote, as one of many similar incidents, the occasion when eight of their men and horses broke up a hysterical crowd of Stuttgart youth 'set alight' by the American rock-and-roller Bill Haley and bent on wrecking the stands in the Killesberg exhibition grounds. When the French President came on a State visit, a top official recorded that the skilful use of police horses saved the watching crowds on the Schlossplatz Stuttgart from being crushed, and that 'men have more respect for the creature than for their own kind.' His report concluded with the moral that 'The Police of a large city should never be afraid of the cost and subsequent expense of police horses'.

Even in Tokyo, teeming with 11,000,000 inhabitants, where the dying art of the geisha girls is being supplanted by the more lucrative one of bar-hostessing, and where modernisation is the keynote, fifteen police horses are on duty amongst the car-jammed streets. Tokyo commuters have to be pushed onto the overflowing rush-hour trains by students hired for the job, and motorists measure distances in driving time instead of kilometres; yet these few horses are employed today amongst all this mechanical hurly-burly and echoes from the past, and are considered particularly effective in preventing traffic and crowd confusion at mass meetings and religious festivals, and irreplaceable for traffic control on the crossings where children commute to and from school.

This mounted police force is descended from the few police officers who had the duty of carrying messages on horseback up to February 1874 when the Metropolitan Police Agency was founded. A regular mounted section was formed soon after this date.

In all probability those original messengers were mounted on Hocaido ponies, the breed native to Japan, near relatives to the Mongolian wild horse and similar in many respects to the fast, hardy Far Eastern type known as the Chinese Pony. Nowadays the police ride half-bred horses of Western origin but domestically produced, good-looking animals suited by size and looks to their various duties which include ceremonial escorts. A trotter and a thoroughbred are also included in the Horse Unit of the Metropolitan Police Department in Tokyo.

The Lesotho police are one of the world's few fully mounted forces. Since the true Basuto Pony is now difficult to find, their 400 horses are country-bred, from the Orange Free State and Natal. They need to be tough to cope with the largely roadless mountainous terrain, and the long patrols that, in May, June and July may be undertaken in heavy snow, with no grazing available and testing conditions.

On the lush tropical island of Trinidad, the eighty police horses that have been controlling crowds and enhancing ceremonial occasions for the past forty years all come from Canada, and are all bred on exactly the same lines, thoroughbred crossed half-bred or cold-blood mares, as those used by the Royal Canadian Mounties. There were no horses in the West Indies, or in America, between the times of the prehistoric herds that roamed the vast plains before becoming extinct, and the Spanish Barb horses and Garrano ponies, and the Minho ponies from Portugal, that Christopher Columbus and Cortez introduced into the New World. In 1493 Columbus brought thirty horses, including ten mares, on the three-month voyage from Cadiz to Hispaniola, or Haiti as it now is; and every ship that subsequently set sail from Spain for the West Indies or New World brought more horses, tied on the open decks with no exercise and no cover from wind or storm. Jamaica was amongst Columbus's West Indian discoveries. He reached it in 1494 and changed its aboriginal name, Xaymaca, Land of Wood and Water, to St Jago. No doubt the twenty locally bred horses that make up the recently formed mounted section of the police in that island are in some part descendants of the survivors from those arduous voyages of long ago.

The decision to form a Mounted Branch of the Jamaica Constabulary was taken in 1958, and in 1960 an officer was recruited on contract from the Birmingham Police to get the branch under way. A mounted troop was actually formed a year later, with a complement of ten sub-officers and constables, and ten horses. At the end of the English officer's contract another officer was seconded from the Royal Canadian Mounted Police to finalise the training of the troop. During this time two sub-officers were sent to Imber Court to imbibe the ways of the Metropolitan Police in England. The horses, all young, have an average height of sixteen hands, and deal with the normal duties of crowd and traffic control, ceremonial escorts and patrolling of the city and public gardens; they also put on an excellent Musical Ride at exhibitions and public functions.

In Italy, a country renowned for horsemanship, Il Carosello Equestre, the Equestrian Tournament, is not exactly a musical ride but a display of precise and skilled training given by men and horses of the Carabinieri. This crack cavalry regiment was formed in 1814 by Vittorio Emanuele 1st, the horse section then being used solely as a personal guard to the head of state. In 1922 the Carabinieri, still an armed force, became solely concerned with public safety. The corps is highly esteemed all over Italy, being known as the *Bene Merita*, the well-deserving; every city and large town has a Carabinieri station. Rome needs no adorning, but like the Horse Guards in Whitehall, the lovely horses and picturesque uniforms of the Presidential Guard at the Quirinale, or a squadron of the Carabinieri clattering through the streets, give just that added flavour.

During the intricate evolutions of Il Carosello Equestre, one

hundred men and horses of the Carabinieri provide not only
an exciting and colourful pageant of past military feats, but also
an exhibition of the high measure of training achieved. The display is not given by a fixed team : the riders, in dark uniforms
enlivened by the blue and purple plumes on their tricorne hats,
are progressively replaced each year by new recruits from the
corps' equestrian schools, a policy that ensures a very high standard of training for men and horses throughout the whole mounted
section. Whether world-famous show jumpers or humbler animals
kept for crowd-control work, all the Carabinieri horses are beautifully schooled and a delight to the eye.

Horse breeding in Italy is carried on in selected studs and
centres organised by the State. A proportion of the horses of the
Carabinieri are of the Italian breeds, Salerno and Calabrese.
Some are cross-bred British thoroughbred or Oriental types and
some come from Sardinia. There are Lippïzanas, the best-known
of all Austrian breeds—famed for the *haute ecolé* they perform at
the Spanish Riding School in Vienna and hailing originally from
Karst near Trieste. The Carabinieri show-jumpers, both human
and equine, are famous all over the world, and the name d'Inzeo
has for years headed the list of the most skilled and successful
competitors. Celebrated horses like the Irish-bred The Rock,
the younger Bells of Clonmell and Bowjack, and Merano and
Posillipo, both bred in Italy, are only kept for competitive work,
but this edict does not apply to their riders. According to a
Roman newspaper some years ago, even the idol of the Italian
public, Captain Raimondo d'Inzeo, momentarily lost some of
the prestige gained by numerous victories in national and international jumping competitions when he was recognised while on
duty in his official capacity. 'We love you as our hero of show-
jumping,' complained his admirers, 'but not when you and your
horse prevent us from taking part in political demonstrations!'

Before the second world war Holland had three police forces
of which the Royal Maréchausée, founded just after the
Napoleonic era, was a form of mounted state police. The present-
day mounted force is also a part of the general state police and
was formed in 1946. One of its peculiarly Dutch duties comes in

Some of the handsome South African police horses are descended from 'Cape Horses'

In Holland during the summer, the police horses (below) help to rescue swimmers in difficulty

Like all mounted policemen, those of Malta are very proud of their fine animals

Police horse and rider help school children in Tokyo to cross the busy streets

spring, when the fields are ablaze with tulips, daffodils and hyacinths, and the mounted police must escort the flower-decked festival floats, restraining their horses from snatching the odd blossom and controlling the gay crowds that fill the streets.

The six sections of mounted police are stationed at different points around the country. The one in The Hague takes on a great deal of summer patrol work amongst the beaches and dunes, with detachments sent to the small islands in the north, to oversee the visitors and tourists camping there, operating on ground that is unusable by motor units: the beaches have patches of quicksand and unexpected holes. Before now the section, cantering merrily along the water's edge for the good of their souls and the horses' legs, have turned to discover a comrade, invisible except for his head and his horse's ears, doing an involuntary 'submarine patrol'. These men carry a thirty to forty-metre lasso attached to their saddles, and many a swimmer in difficulty owes his life to the Dutch mounted policeman's expertise in throwing a life-line. When a child is floundering helplessly, man and horse go in to the rescue together, the rider swimming alongside his horse, one hand on the saddle pommel, the other grabbing the child as the trained animal turns obediently to make for shore.

This Dutch mounted section includes a few young men, sons of farmers who can ride and want to work with horses, but the majority are middle-aged men who were in the Maréchausée or cavalry before the war. All have done a few years as foot police before joining the modern mounted force. They are an able, efficient, horse-loving crowd, hearty eaters and hard-headed drinkers with a robust appreciation of the funny side of life. Men and horses alike are extremely popular with the public, and there is the usual trouble with horses spoiled by too many titbits from admirers, so that now and then they catch their riders unawares and break ranks at inopportune moments on catching the mere sniff of an ice cream or a bag of sweets. Nothing comes much amiss.

One squadron soaked to the skin after providing a royal escort, and caught out by the General as they dried themselves off in a convenient café, thought nothing of springing to attention in their socks and underpants, ignoring the very apparent presence of a couple of bottles of gin. On their Colonel's birthday, as the mounted police were returning through the dunes to The Hague after a morning's training, the commander felt that man and horse had earned their fun. 'Charge!' he shouted, and 'Gallop!' and away they went, spreading out up and down the dunes, hilariously belting along until they managed to halt at last—and count empty saddles and missing hats, and the irretrievable loss of a set of false teeth.

Before the war the cavalry were all mounted on Irish horses, but nowadays various types are used, Czech horses, French thoroughbreds, the offspring of German Holstein and Trakehners crossed with home-bred mares, and a large percentage of a Dutch breed, the Gelderland. Like the German police horses, they are ridden in snaffles and dropped nosebands, the saddles now being of English pattern, superseding the former cavalry saddle 'A', which was mounted on four little curved wooden appendages, like miniature water-skis, with a folded blanket under all, and a proven reputation for comfort and safety.

The horses are schooled on dressage lines and, needless to remark, their wellbeing comes first with their riders—as one quartermaster of the Amsterdam police discovered to his cost when the mounted section came to town for the coronation of Queen Juliana. They were quartered on the local police force who made special provision for them at a café—and regretted their hospitality when it was reported that three stable guards had 'eaten' forty-five bread rolls with butter at a single sitting!

CHAPTER TEN

POLICE-HORSE 'CHARACTERS'

ALL around the world the mounted police forces cherish the horse 'characters' which enliven their ranks, and have tales to tell of endearing, successful or eccentric equine personalities from the past. Many of these horses are remembered for their prowess in the field of sport.

In Britain during the thirties, the pride of the Metropolitan force was Energy, a mare that would jump six foot, over anything from a motor car to a jet of water squirted from a hose. Today there are many like Moira, a liver-chestnut white-faced mare and the sergeant's horse at Kings Cross Police Station, animals that combine a good working record with being real 'sports horses', fast and skilled in different competitions. Some are better at one event, some at another; a few, like Moira, are a bit temperamental when it comes to Best Trained Horse classes which involve 'nuisances'. Pennine Way and Cheviot Lad uphold the honours for the mounted branch of the West Riding Constabulary, Top Twig and Red King did so in the past for Salford City. Walbrook was the star of the City of London Police until he met with an accident show-jumping, and Ethel belongs to Brixton, in London, as mentioned in Chapter 2.

In fact, though Ethel may be stabled at Brixton and emerge from there to perform all the duties demanded of a first-class, fully experienced police horse, she belongs to the whole of the Metropolitan force. She is all things to every Metropolitan police-man, the greatest all-round police horse remembered; 'a great character and a real Christian!' A good doer—'keeps fat on fresh air'—she thrives on work, and remains as round and hard as an apple. Being grey, Ethel has to be washed every day, but has never had so much as a cold. There are few, if any, shows around the country which include a police class in which she has not competed, and from the day in 1955 when she first won the King George V Challenge Cup for Best Trained Police Horse in the United Kingdom, she has gone from strength to strength. The list of Ethel's successes would fill a page. Her greatest asset, of course, is her wonderful temperament. She can take part in all the flat-out galloping excitement of a tent-pegging event, within an hour appear as the perfectly schooled, placid, co-operative Best Trained Horse of the day, and on street patrol stand untended in the worst of traffic while her rider copes with an 'incident'. I met Ethel at Great Scotland Yard, and one look at this venerable, essentially feminine creature with long, rather woolly ears and expressive kindly eyes, endorsed what they say of her : 'Ethel wouldn't harm a fly—you could put your bed down beside her in the stall and sleep as safe and sound as in your own bedroom.'

Blenheim, the big black horse stationed at Southwark, London, has won rosettes and cups in his time at Richmond, but he is into his twenties now, still fully operational but confining his more public appearances to ceremonial work. Blenheim was one of the black police horses that headed the funeral cortège for Sir Winston Churchill. He has attended the Trooping the Colour for sixteen or seventeen years now, for a long time past having carried Field Marshal Earl Alexander—who reckons Blenheim amongst his friends, and greets him when they pass in the street. This horse has a dignified, noble bearing, but that did not prevent him one day, when his rider's attention was distracted, from snicking the carnation from the buttonhole of an immaculately dressed gentleman and munching it with relish under the eye if its indignant would-be wearer.

Some police horses have eccentricities that are very much their own, like the mare at Great Scotland Yard who will only enter her box forwards by taking an enormous kangaroo leap—but who will go in backwards as quietly as a lamb. Dude, of Troop 'C', New York, dislikes his bridle. No one knows why, but occasionally when his patrolman returns from lunch he finds a bridle still hitched to a post and no horse; he then has the embarrassment of searching Central Park for an undressed Dude—much to the amusement of the public. Then, for fifteen years Benny of the Dutch Mounted Police has been ridden by the commanding officer on escort to the Queen of the Netherlands' carriage when she drives out for the annual opening of Parliament. Fifteen years ago Benny came out of the palace gates for the first time to meet the beat of drums and waving of flags, and in particular to a flapping encounter with an enormous regimental flag on his off side, dipped just as the entourage emerged. Benny, aged only five, took a poor view of it; he pricked his ears and bunched his quarters and his rider thought, 'Oho! Here we go!' He pushed the horse on to the bit, however, and used his legs, and they sidled by. And every year since then, Benny has treated his rider to the same little display, not because he now minds the regimental flag at all but because, as the commanding officer puts it, 'It's more of a kind of play we do together!' Adding thoughtfully, 'I like things like that. . . .'

Pueblo of the New York City Police was, or possibly still is, famous for his addiction to sleep. His rider indignantly refuted the suggestion that Pueblo was in fact bone-idle, stressing that he was a mighty fine animal that had merely achieved the art of relaxing. Anyone could sit or stretch out on the horse when he was napping: Pueblo could not care less. But if offered sugar he would manage to lift his head and accept it, before resuming his slumbers. On several occasions Pueblo has been reported dead by conscientious rookies who came upon him sprawled out in his stall. Dusty, the twenty-eight-year-old Southend police horse who died in retirement in 1967, is remembered not only for his kind temperament but also for his penchant for ice-cream, a delicacy to which he helped himself, even when on duty, whenever the opportunity occurred.

Somewhere in Holland is an ex-police horse called Blackie who has the edge on the Southend horse when it comes to age; thirty if he is a day, Blackie was also retired but is still very much alive, and now the prized and pampered mount of a spry old gentle-man in his eighties who climbs aboard him with the aid of a stepladder. The Dutch Mounted Police, like the Metropolitan, normally have their old horses put down on retirement, but sometimes an exception to the rule is made if a first-class suitable home is offered, with a guarantee that the horse will not change hands.

Before the Metropolitan rule came in, retired horses were occasionally sold to the public, and a Hampstead parlour-maid once spent £12 on a brown gelding after it was removed from police work. In those days it was distinct 'one-up-manship' for anyone 'in service' to own a horse, but the poor girl's triumph was short-lived. She was injured and her horse killed when a car ran into them—whether the £176 she received for personal injuries and loss of horse entirely compensated for her misfortunes, no one seems to know.

Other mounted police would surely welcome horses as helpful as a couple that at one time belonged to the South African force. Chummy was a true police horse in every sense of the word; he would not only assist in the searches for unauthorised liquor stills, but was usually the first to smell them out. Should he, however, be denied what he considered a fair share of the resulting booty, Chummy immediately went on strike and refused to be of any further assistance. Jimmy was a horse of the old school, well versed in many ways not actually laid down in the training manual. At that time police students took guard duty in the stables at night, a wearying responsibility only made possible by taking an occasional forty winks curled up in Jimmy's manger. This breach of the regulations could be safely indulged because Jimmy could be relied on to wake any sleeper with far from gentle nudges of his nose directly he heard the measured tread of the approaching duty sergeant.

The London Metropolitan Police are always on the lookout for any of their horses that might one day be suitable for the Queen or Prince Philip to ride at the Trooping the Colour. Some potentials never make the grade, but three or four likely horses are normally in the running.

On the Coronation Year crown piece, and on the Great Seal of Lancaster, the Queen is depicted riding the police horse Win-

ston. This big chestnut, mentioned in Chapter 3, was ridden by
King George VI on several of his official birthday parades, and
then by his daughter, first as Princess Elizabeth and then for
some years after she became Queen. Winston, a half-brother to
the celebrated international show-jumper Foxhunter, was a big
horse with a fine majestic presence that appealed to the public.
He thoroughly enjoyed ceremonial parades, and his only dis-
advantage was an ultra-sensitive skin, a drawback that on two
separate occasions made him fidgety during the long wait on
Horseguards Parade, once when a cloud of thunder-flies began
biting beyond endurance, once when a tiny ruckle in the ornamental saddle-cloth started to irritate. Winston had to be destroyed after slipping and injuring himself in the street in 1957.

His successor, Imperial, is another chestnut gelding who as
an unbroken three-year old also came from Yorkshire. Imperial
is three-quarter bred, a good-looking chestnut with much quality
and an essentially kind if gay disposition. His manners on parade
have always been excellent, and he too is a horse that appreci-
ates all the pomp and military circumstance that attend the
Trooping the Colour; but he is not altogether an easy ride. Both
by breeding and temperament he needs tactful handling. He
'takes hold' even at the walk, and the Queen herself, though she
has ridden him with enjoyment for many years, has said that
in the indoor riding-school at Buckingham Palace Imperial pulls
harder than any horse she knows. Also, Imperial has always suffered from weak feet. Despite every care and special shoes designed by the late Professor McCunn of the Royal Veterinary
College, he has once or twice been prevented by lameness from
appearing on parade. His place has been taken by Doctor, a
kindly grey horse with the large eyes and hint of a 'dished' profile
that suggests Arabian blood somewhere in his veins. In his day
Doctor has been a most versatile animal, excellent alike as royal
escort, at work in the East End or taking part in the Activity
Ride; but he is no longer in his first youth. The Queen last rode
him in 1966, but will probably not do so again.

In 1965, during the month of almost daily side-saddle riding
that the Queen—who otherwise rides astride—puts in before

the day of the Trooping, she enjoyed taking turn and turn about in the Palace riding-school with Imperial and a young horse called Neill. Neill is a big brown horse of different conformation from Imperial, and maybe lacking a little of the chestnut's quality, but with presence and a wonderful temperament. Even at that time, if he lacked Imperial's experience and dependability on the parade ground, Neill was a much easier ride in the school and went well for Mrs Archer Houblon at the rehearsal of the Trooping. He is also a character, a Houdini where door-fastenings are concerned, and takes a mischievous delight in letting himself out of his own box, wandering across the gangway to incite a couple of neighbours to pull faces at each other, and then strolling back to his own quarters, to watch with interest their unavailing efforts to get to grips. Prince Philip rode Neill at the Trooping in 1966 and found that he deported himself well but, influenced by the behaviour of others, was inclined to break from the required walk. A year later the Duke reverted to his well-tried mare Linnhe, and the Queen rode Neill, then ten years old and achieving an impressive and impeccable standard.

Without ever aspiring to the chief role, many Metropolitan Police horses attend the Trooping year after year and become familiar public figures. The big old horse Fairway, the Duke of Gloucester's mount for many seasons, was famous for his 'straddle'. Perfect in manners and in standing, Fairway believed in an even distribution of weight and used to shift his legs out at an angle to attain it. He also saw no reason why he and Prince Philip's horse should be stationed half a length behind the Queen's, and at intervals, to the Queen's amusement, used an unobtrusive shuffle to try and remedy the position. Like Blenheim, the aged grey Alamein is stabled at Southwark, and was bought in 1947 as a four-year-old. His now white figure, his long slobbery tongue protruding from between his lips, is as well known at the Trooping the Colour as in the Lord Mayor's Procession, where for many years he has carried the City Marshal. No longer ridden by Prince Philip, Alamein still attends the Trooping, carrying a royal groom and ready to be handed over as a replacement horse to any VIP in need.

Officer in charge of the Mounted Section of the New South Wales police

Lesotho police sometimes patrol for weeks on end, and mules carry provisions for them and their sturdy, native-bred ponies

In Bahrein the police stallions are bred at the Palace of the ruling Sheikh

The Teheran mounted police fire from the saddle, and their stallions are trained to stand like rocks

Bedouin of the Camel Corps police the borders of Jordan

Wiry little Jordanian horses at the police post of the Inn of the Good Samaritan, not far from Jerusalem

A replacement horse was very nearly required with some urgency in Australia when the Queen paid a visit in 1954. The mounted police had a smart, eye-catching escort of cream-coloured palominos drawn up on parade at the airport, and one of them dropped dead; but the old horse was such a perfect gentleman that he waited until everyone had gone by before gently collapsing beneath his rider.

If ever a horse saw history in the making, that one was Quicksilver, Sir Percy Laurie's famous ex-warhorse. In his official capacity as Assistant Commissioner between 1919 and 1936, the grey horse's master attended every ceremony of note that came within his province in London's Metropolitan area, and whenever practicable Quicksilver went too. During those years he carried Field Marshal Lord Trenchard on his last appearance at the Trooping the Colour, followed in the funeral procession of King George V, and in that for the victims of the R101 disaster. He was present in the ring at the International Horse Show at Olympia in 1920, 1934 and 1936, won the King's Cup at the Richmond Royal Horse Show and was awarded first prize for the Best Trained Police Horse at Olympia. Through the years Quicksilver collected £306 in his nosebag in aid of the rebuilding of the Royal Veterinary College, Camden Town, where a loose box is dedicated to his memory. Two years after retiring with his owner to Wiltshire the grey was out hunting, but when war broke out again and Major General Sir Percy Laurie rejoined, to serve once more as Provost Marshal of the United Kingdom and Commandant of Military Police from 1940 to 1943, Quicksilver remained in well-earned peace until his end in his thirty-fourth year.

Quicksilver was involved in war many years ago now, but the little Jordanian mare that I watched being groomed in the police compound at the Inn of the Good Samaritan may, with her sergeant rider, have been swept into the turmoil and tragedy of the June 1967 Arab-Israeli war. I do not know, nor ever shall, whether she and the friendly sergeant are still alive, but I shall never forget the short term of our acquaintance. She was small and wiry, an Arabian type well up to the combined weight of the sergeant and his accoutrements, capable of covering long distances over the roughest ground, sure-footed, frugal to feed and trained to make do with the minimum of water. She had never before been ridden by a European, let alone a woman, and as previously described thought little of the idea. I was beginning to consider it an overrated one myself, by the time we had emerged crabwise out of the compound on to a track leading to the Jerusalem to Jericho road. I had some thought of riding up the steep rock-strewn hillside behind the police station where a low black Bedouin tent crouched in a hollow, but each time, riding two-handed in true pony-club style, I so much as touched the mare's mouth, she shot her head back on to my nose and proceeded in a series of nerve-racking bounds: it seemed advisable to remain on the level. We reached the end of the track, where one look at the lorries roaring past on their way to the Holy City convinced me of the need for retreat, and returned to the police station more by good luck than good judgment.

This was the moment to come to terms, and I dropped my reins and began to talk to her. The mare knew as little of English as I knew of Arabic, but the tone was right and communication established. We both relaxed and set off again, within the constricted space of the sand-strewn compound, and as I realised what I should have known in the first place, that the little chestnut responded to neck-reining, she began to twist and turn to my slightest wish, light and active as a supple cat. The heat went out of the day. Beyond the brown, dry hills stretching into the distance the sky took fire, slashed in streaks of crimson and orange, and I realized guiltily that absorbed in each other's company the mare and I had forgotten our small audience of patient if justifiably puzzled driver and policemen, and now the night was there.

They come in all shapes and sizes, these horses. Irish Hunter, Turkoman stallion, Native Pony, Hanoverian gelding, English Thoroughbred and Arabian mare, dispersed in small units throughout the world, willing, obedient, and unknowingly helping to keep what mankind expends its energies in trying to break —the peace and order by which we live. All of them, despite their diverse appearance, are descendants of the Ice Age horse, the true Mongolian wild horse which lived for thousands of years on the steppe lands of the western Gobi Desert, and of which about a hundred now survive in zoos such as Washington and Whipsnade, Paris and Prague, Chicago and Amsterdam. These animals were only discovered in 1881, and a few may still have escaped the hunters. If any do remain in their natural habitat, they and their zoo-bred relatives are the only authentically wild horses in the world—stocky, hardy little animals of twelve to fourteen hands, dun-coloured, dorsal and zebra striped with a stand-up mane.

Rated by human levels or even that of monkeys and dogs, horses are not particularly intelligent animals; if they were they would long ago have realised by how many times their physical strength surpasses our own, and seen through the tricks we employ to control them. But they are sensitive, highly strung creatures, capable of putting great trust in the man who wins their confidence and, despite the pundits, liable to become very attached to their owner. They have excellent memories, one of the factors making it possible to train them to the high standards achieved today, and they are very responsive to human emotion. This trait, combined with the realisation that horses react to instinct but not to reasoning, as we undersand it, explains the behaviour of a horse bewildered by an inexpert rider. Few horses set out deliberately to do wrong, but they may well play up because of a rider's inability to make his message plain.

It is easy to lay down set rules of equine behaviour, to state that in certain circumstances 'horses do this, horses do that', and that they should all be treated in such and such a way, but as always generalisation is a tricky business. People such as mounted policemen who work with horses know that different animals can be as dissimilar as chalk from cheese and accept the challenge of finding out what makes each animal tick. That is in fact one of the reasons why, throughout the world, the ranks of the mounted police are always filled.

Maybe it is also one of the reasons why police horses may survive in the future. No machine can ever possess the endearing

and unexpected idiosyncrasies that belong to creatures of flesh
and blood; and mankind still needs the humanising experience
of dealing with sentient animals other than those of his own
species. A policeman with a motor-bike or car can be proud of
the machine's performance, and is indispensable in today's world;
but he can never establish the inter-dependent relationship with
his vehicle that the mounted policeman has with his horse—and
no machinery of the law, either now or in the future, can evoke
the response from the public won by a police horse.

INDEX

The names of individual horses are printed in italics

Abdullah, Amir (King), 98, 99, 103, 105
Akhal Tekeh horses, 96, 100, 149
Alamein, 71, 172
Alkhalifah, Sheikh, 149
Ambassadors, presenting credentials, 61, 62
Amos, 83
Anglo-Norman horses, 156
Arabian dromedaries, 100
Arabian horses, 97, 103, 150, 151, 177, 178
Archer Houblon, Mrs, 27, 50, 57, 172
Australian walers, 122, 151

Bachelor Gay, 37
Bahrein Police, 149, 150
Basuto ponies, 152
Bedouin, the, 34, 98, 99, 100, 103, 104, 178
Bells of Clonmell, 162
Benny, 169
Bexley, Miss, 75
Billy, 26, 27
Birmingham Police, 70, 161
Blackfeet Confederacy, 137, 139
Blackfoot Indians, 135, 137-40
Blackie, 169
Blackpool Police, 22
Blenheim, 43, 168, 172
Boston Police, 81-3
Bowjack, 162
Bow Street, 11, 28, 32
Bow Street Horse Patrol, 12-15, 19, 113, 121, 151

Bow Street Runners, 11, 121
Brighton Police, 75
Brig o' Dee, 63
Bristol Police, 41, 70, 75, 76
Brixton Police Station, 41, 64, 167
Bushrangers, Australia, 108, 111, 116, 117

Calabrese horses, 162
Camels, 100, 101, 102, 114; Camel Corps, 100, 102, 114
Cannon Row Police Station, 58
Cape horses, 151
Carabinieri, the, Italy, 41, 161, 162
'Charlies', 11, 14, 69
Cherry Grove, 43
Cheviot Lad, 167
Chinese ponies, 160
Chummy, 170
City of London Police, 24, 32, 33, 44, 56, 63, 68-72, 167
City Marshal, 57, 71, 172
Cleveland Bays, 55, 61, 159
Cobham, 57
Collar chains, 57
Country patrols, 16, 40, 51, 64, 65, 68, 72, 75, 76, 82, 158, 159, 165
Crowd control, 15, 16, 20, 25-9, 32, 57, 62, 76, 82, 88, 96, 97, 121, 124, 149, 153, 154, 159, 160, 161
Crowfoot, Chief, 137-9
Custer, General, 138

Darashoori horses, 96
Desert Patrol, Jordan, 99, 100
Diamond Jubilee, the, 20, 142, 143

182   INDEX

Dickens' Medal, 31
d'Inzeo, Raimonde, 41, 162
Doctor, 58, 171
Dooley, Sergeant, 81, 83
Downs Ranger, Sussex, 77-9
Dude, 168-9
Dusty, 169
Dutch Mounted Police, 25, 56-8, 162, 165-6, 169-70

Eastbourne Police, 77
Edinburgh Police, 75, 76-7
Emma, 52
Energy, 167
Ethel, 41, 167-8

Fairfax, 75
Fairway, 172
Faisal, King, 60
Feisal, Emir, 98, 104
Fielding, Henry, 11
Fielding, John, 11, 12, 107
Fleur, 153
Fort MacLeod, Canada, 136-7, 141
Fort Walsh, Canada, 147

Garde Républicaine, France, 155-6
Gelderland horses, 166
Generous Star, 37
Glasgow Police, 31, 79
Glubb, Lt-General Sir John, 99
Gold Police, Australia, 115
Gorleston Palace, Teheran, 94
Great Scotland Yard, 43, 55, 58, 63, 168
Grootdam stud, South Africa, 150-2
Guardia Civil, Spain, 156-7

Hammersmith Police Station, 51, 64
Handcuffs, 121
Hanoverian horses, 159, 178
Harmony, 56
Highwaymen, 12, 14, 108
Hocaido ponies, 160
Holstein horses, 158-9, 166
Hudson Bay Company, 132, 134, 137, 138, 140

Hull (Kingston upon Hull) Police, 75
Hussein, King, 98, 103
Huwaitet Tribe, 99, 100

Ikhwan, the, 60, 99, 100
Imber Court training centre, 27, 32, 33-53, 55, 66, 70, 90, 119, 152
Imperial, 31, 32, 58, 171, 172
Indians, Red, 130-3, 136-40, 142
Iran, 76, 93, 94-8, 149

Jamaica Constabulary, 161
Jimmy, 170
Jordan, 33, 34, 60, 98-105, 114, 149
Jordan, 89
Joseph, 80, 81
Juma, Sub. Inspector Z., 149
Jumbo, 79

Kim, 75
King, 63
King's Cross Police Station, 56, 64, 167
Kingston upon Hull Police, 75

Lancashire Constabulary, 75
Laurie, Lt-Col Sir Percy, 23-4, 25, 29, 30, 33, 34, 43, 144, 177
Lesotho Police, 33, 160
Lincoln Prince, 37
Linnhe, 58, 172
Lippïzanas horses, 162
Liverpool Police, 75
London Police: *see* Metropolitan Police; City of London Police

Maister, 75
Malta Police, 33, 158
Manchester Police, 43, 75, 76
Mark, 77
Merano, 162
Metropolitan Police, London, 11, 14, 22 *et seq*, 30 *et seq*, 41, 51, 52, 55, 57, 59, 60, 64, 68, 96, 105, 144, 167, 170
Metropolitan Police Horse Show, 42, 71

Milton, 43
Moira, 167
Mongolian wild horses, 179
Morgan horses, 83, 89
Mounted Park-Keeper Force, London, 68
Mounties, Canadian, *see* Royal Canadian Mounted Police; North West Mounted Police
Musical Ride: Metropolitan, 41-3; Canadian, 129-31; Jamaican, 161

Native Police, Australia, 113, 114
Neill, 172
Newcastle upon Tyne Police, 72, 80
New South Wales Police, 108, 111-13, 115-20, 155
New York Police, 27, 55, 76, 80, 81, 83, 84-93, 155, 168-9
New Zealand, early history, 124, 125; Police, 125, 126
Northern Territory Police, Australia, 114
North West Mounted Police, Canada, 130, 131, 134-6, 140-2, 144, 147-9; *see also* Royal Canadian Mounted Police
Norwegian Police, 56, 153-4
Nuisance training, 43-4, 49, 120

Otisville, New York, 93
Ottawa, 130, 132, 134

Palestine Police, 104, 105
Paris Police, 155
Parry, Bowen, 142-4, 148-9
Patriarch, 89
Peake, Lt-Col, 98
Peel, Sir Robert, 14, 15, 19, 64, 68-9
Peelers, 16
Pennine Way, 167
Percheron horses, 150
Persian Arab horses, 96
'Persuit Horses', 11, 15, 32
Peterloo, 15
Posillipo, 162
Potts, Jerry, 136

Prince, 80
Princess Pat, 77-9
Pueblo, 169

Queensland Police, Australia, 120
Quicksilver, 23-4, 30, 177

Ranger, Downs, Sussex, 77-9
Redbreasts, 13, 16
Redcliffe, 42
Red King, 167
Regal, 31
Richard, 89
Richmond Show, 41, 43, 44, 177
Riel, Louis, 139
Rival, 89
Robin, 41
Rochester Row Police Station, 51
Rock, The, 41, 162
Royal Canadian Mounted Police, 20, 129-131, 137, 139, 141, 143, 147, 160, 161; *see also* North West Mounted Police
Royal Mews, London, 54, 55, 57, 59, 61; Windsor, 96; Farahabad, 96
Royal Scots Greys, 23, 144, 148
Rusty, 83, 89

Salerno horses, 162
Salford Police, 43, 75, 76, 167
Saudi Arabia, 33, 60, 99-101
Saxa, 89
Scorey, PC, 26
Selbourne, 153
Shammah, 103
Shawn, 81
Sitting Bull, Chief, 138, 139
Sioux Indians, 138, 139
Snodgrass, 75
South African Police, 33, 150-3
South Australian Police, 114, 120-1, 130
Southampton Police, 23, 76
Southend Police, 169
Southwark Police Station, 43, 52, 64, 168

Stüttgart Police, 27, 158-9
Swedish Police, 154-5

Tasmanian Police, 112
Teheran Police, 27, 95-8, 144
Templar, 70
Thoroughbreds, 156, 159, 160, 162, 178
Tiger, 152
Tokyo Police, 27, 159-60
Tom, 77
Tommy, 58
Top Twig, 167
Trinidad Police, 160
Trooping the Colour, 32, 57-8, 63, 72, 168, 170, 172, 177
Turk, 152-3

Turkoman horses, 96, 178
Tyra, 153

Victoria Police, Australia, 112, 113, 115, 117, 121-4

Walbrook, 70, 167
Waler horses, 122, 151
Wandsworth Police Station, 52
Warrior, 23
Watson, 89
Western Australia Police, 114, 121
West Riding Constabulary, York-shire, 42, 76, 167
Wilberforce, William, 75
Winston, 31, 58, 171

WILSHIRE HORSE LOVERS' LIBRARY

_____APPALOOSA HORSE *Bill & Dona Richardson*   2.00

_____ARABIAN HORSE *Reginald S. Summerhays*   2.00

_____AT THE HORSE SHOW *Margaret Cabell Self*   2.00

_____BACK-YARD FOAL *Peggy Jett Pittenger*   2.00

_____BACK-YARD HORSE *Peggy Jett Pittenger*   2.00

_____DRESSAGE A Study of the Finer Points in Riding *Henry Wynmalen*   2.00

_____EQUITATION *Jean Froissard*   2.00

_____FUN OF RAISING A COLT *Rubye & Frank Griffith*   2.00

_____FUN ON HORSEBACK *Margaret Cabell Self*   2.00

_____HORSE OWNER'S CONCISE GUIDE *Elsie V. Hanauer*   2.00

_____HORSE SELECTION & CARE FOR BEGINNERS *George H. Conn*   2.00

_____HORSEBACK RIDING MADE FUN & EASY *Sue Henderson Coen*   2.00

_____HORSES Their Selection, Care & Handling *Margaret Cabell Self*   2.00

_____POLICE HORSES *Judith Campbell*   2.00

_____PROBLEM HORSES *Reginald S. Summerhays*

   Tested Guide for Curing Most Common & Serious Horse Behavior Habits. 2.00

_____SCHOOLING YOUR YOUNG HORSE *George Wheatley*   2.00

_____TRAIL HORSES & TRAIL RIDING *Anne & Perry Westbrook*   2.00

_____WONDERFUL WORLD OF PONIES *Peggy Jett Pittenger*   2.00

_____YOUR WESTERN HORSE *Nelson C. Nye*   2.00

Special Imported Book

_____THE LIPIZZANERS AND THE SPANISH RIDING SCHOOL *W. Reuter*   2.00

The books listed above can be obtained from your book dealer
or directly from Wilshire Book Company. When ordering, please remit.
Send for our free 208 page illustrated catalog of self-improvement books.

Wilshire Book Company

12015 Sherman Road, No. Hollywood, California 91605

WILSHIRE
Self-Improvement
LIBRARY

_____ABILITY TO LOVE *by Dr. Allan Fromme* $2.00
_____ACT YOUR WAY TO SUCCESSFUL LIVING *Neil & Margaret Rau* 2.00
_____ADVANCED TECHNIQUES OF HYPNOSIS *Melvin Powers* 1.00
_____ANIMAL HYPNOSIS *Dr. F. A. Völgyesi* 2.00
_____ASTROLOGY: A FASCINATING HISTORY *P. Naylor* 2.00
_____ASTROLOGY: HOW TO CHART YOUR HOROSCOPE *Max Heindel* 2.00
_____ASTROLOGY: YOUR PERSONAL SUN-SIGN GUIDE *Beatrice Ryder* 2.00
_____ASTROLOGY FOR EVERYDAY LIVING *Janet Harris* 2.00
_____ASTROLOGY GUIDE TO GOOD HEALTH *Alexandra Kayhle* 2.00
_____ASTROLOGY MADE EASY *by Astarte* 2.00
_____ASTROLOGY MADE PRACTICAL *Alexandra Kayhle* 2.00
_____ASTROLOGY, ROMANCE, YOU AND THE STARS *Anthony Novell* 2.00
_____CHAMPIONSHIP CHECKERS IN TEN EASY LESSONS *Tom Wiswell* 2.00
_____CHESS IN TEN EASY LESSONS *Grandmaster Larry Evans* 2.00
_____CHESS MADE EASY *Milton L. Hanauer* 1.00
_____CHESS PROBLEMS FOR BEGINNERS *edited by Fred Reinfeld* 1.00
_____CHESS SECRETS REVEALED *Fred Reinfeld* 1.00
_____CHESS TACTICS FOR BEGINNERS *edited by Fred Reinfeld* 1.00
_____CHESS THEORY & PRACTICE *W. Ritson Morry & W. Melville Mitchell* 2.00
_____CHILDBIRTH WITH HYPNOSIS *William S. Kroger, M.D.* 2.00
_____COIN COLLECTING FOR BEGINNERS *by Burton Hobson & Fred Reinfeld* 2.00
_____CONCENTRATION—A Guide to Mental Mastery *Mouni Sadhu* 2.00
_____CONVERSATION MADE EASY *Elliot Russell* 1.00
_____CYBERNETICS WITHIN US *Y. Saparina* 2.00
_____DOCTOR PYGMALION *Maxwell Maltz, M.D.* 2.00
_____DREAMS & OMENS REVEALED *Fred Gettings* 2.00
_____DR. LINDNER'S SPECIAL WEIGHT CONTROL METHOD *P. Lindner* 1.00
_____DYNAMIC THINKING *Melvin Powers* 1.00
_____EAT, THINK & BE SLENDER *Leonid Kotkin, M.D.* 2.00
_____ENCYCLOPEDIA OF MODERN SEX &
          LOVE TECHNIQUES *by R. Macandrew* 2.00
_____EXAM SECRET *Dennis B. Jackson* 1.00
_____FORTUNE TELLING WITH CARDS *P. Foli* 2.00
_____GAYELORD HAUSER'S NEW GUIDE TO INTELLIGENT REDUCING 2.00
_____GOULD'S GOLD & SILVER GUIDE TO COINS *Maurice Gould* 2.00
_____GROW RICH WHILE YOU SLEEP *Ben Sweetland* 2.00
_____GUIDE TO DEVELOPING YOUR POTENTIAL *Herbert A. Otto, Ph.D.* 2.00
_____GUIDE TO HAPPINESS *Dr. Maxwell S. Cagan* 2.00
_____GUIDE TO LIVING IN BALANCE *Frank S. Caprio, M.D.* 2.00
_____GUIDE TO RATIONAL LIVING *Albert Ellis, Ph.D. & R. Harper, Ph.D.* 2.00
_____GUIDE TO SUCCESSFUL LIVING *Joe D. Batten & Leonard C. Hudson* 2.00
_____GUIDE TO SUCCESSFUL MARRIAGE *Drs. Albert Ellis & R. Harper* 2.00

WILSHIRE
Self-Improvement
LIBRARY

_____HANDWRITING ANALYSIS MADE EASY *John Marley*   2.00
_____HARMONICA PLAYING FOR FUN & PROFIT *Hal Leighton*   1.00
_____HEALING POWER OF HERBS *May Bethel*   2.00
_____HELP YOURSELF TO BETTER SIGHT *Margaret Darst Corbett*   2.00
_____HELPING YOURSELF WITH APPLIED PSYCHOLOGY *R. Henderson*   2.00
_____HELPING YOURSELF WITH PSYCHIATRY *Frank S. Caprio, M.D.*   2.00
_____HERBS FOR HEALTH How To Grow & Use Them *Louise Evans Doole*   2.00
_____HOW TO ATTRACT GOOD LUCK *A. H. Z. Carr*   2.00
_____HOW TO DEVELOP A BETTER SPEAKING VOICE *M. Hellier*   1.00
_____HOW TO DEVELOP A WINNING PERSONALITY *by Martin Panzer*   2.00
_____HOW TO DEVELOP AN EXCEPTIONAL MEMORY *Young and Gibson*   2.00
_____HOW TO IMPROVE YOUR BRIDGE *Alfred Sheinwold*   2.00
_____HOW TO LIVE A RICHER & FULLER LIFE *Rabbi Edgar F. Magnin*   2.00
_____HOW TO MAKE MONEY IN REAL ESTATE *Stanley L. McMichael*   2.00
_____HOW TO OVERCOME YOUR FEARS *M. P. Leahy, M.D.*   2.00
_____HOW TO SLEEP WITHOUT PILLS *Dr. David F. Tracy*   1.00
_____HOW TO SOLVE YOUR SEX PROBLEMS
        WITH SELF-HYPNOSIS *F. Caprio, M.D.*   2.00
_____HOW TO STOP SMOKING THRU SELF-HYPNOSIS *Leslie M. LeCron*   2.00
_____HOW TO UNDERSTAND YOUR DREAMS *Geoffrey A. Dudley*   2.00
_____HOW TO USE AUTO-SUGGESTION EFFECTIVELY *John Duckworth*   2.00
_____HOW TO WIN AT BRIDGE *by Edwin Kantar*   2.00
_____HOW TO WIN AT CHECKERS *Fred Reinfeld*   2.00
_____HOW TO WIN AT POCKET BILLIARDS *Edward D. Knuchell*   2.00
_____HOW TO WIN AT POKER *Terence Reese & Anthony T. Watkins*   1.00
_____HOW YOU CAN BOWL BETTER USING SELF-HYPNOSIS *Jack Heise*   2.00
_____HOW YOU CAN HAVE CONFIDENCE AND POWER *Les Giblin*   2.00
_____HOW YOU CAN PLAY BETTER GOLF USING SELF-HYPNOSIS *Heise*   2.00
_____HOW YOU CAN STOP SMOKING PERMANENTLY *Ernest Caldwell*   1.00
_____HYPNOSIS AND SELF-HYPNOSIS *Bernard Hollander, M.D.*   2.00
_____HYPNOTISM *Carl Sextus*   2.00
_____HYPNOTISM & ESP *Simeon Edmunds*   2.00
_____HYPNOTISM MADE PRACTICAL *Louis Orton*   2.00
_____HYPNOTISM REVEALED *Melvin Powers*   1.00
_____HYPNOTISM TODAY *Leslie LeCron & Jean Bordeaux, Ph.D.*   2.00
_____HYPNOTIST'S CASE BOOK *Alex Erskine*   1.00
_____I WILL *Ben Sweetland*   2.00
_____IMPOTENCE & FRIGIDITY *Edwin W. Hirsch, M.D.*   2.00
_____INCREASE YOUR LEARNING POWER *Geoffrey A. Dudley*   1.00
_____JUGGLING MADE EASY *Rudolf Dittrich*   1.00
_____LEFT-HANDED PEOPLE *Michael Barsley*   2.00
_____LSD—THE AGE OF MIND *Bernard Roseman*   2.00

WILSHIRE
Self-Improvement
LIBRARY

_____MAGIC IN YOUR MIND *U. S. Andersen*   2.00
_____MAGIC OF NUMBERS *Robert Tocquet*   2.00
_____MAGIC OF THINKING BIG *Dr. David J. Schwartz*   2.00
_____MAGIC POWER OF YOUR MIND *Walter M. Germain*   2.00
_____MASTER KEYS TO SUCCESS, POPULARITY & PRESTIGE *C. W. Bailey*   2.00
_____MEDICAL HYPNOSIS HANDBOOK *Drs. Van Pelt, Ambrose, Newbold*   2.00
_____MENTAL POWER THRU SLEEP SUGGESTION *Melvin Powers*   1.00
_____MENTAL TELEPATHY EXPLAINED *Hereward Carrington*   .50
_____MIND OVER PLATTER *Peter G. Lindner, M.D.*   2.00
_____MODERN HYPNOSIS *Lesley Kuhn & Salvatore Russo, Ph.D.*   2.00
_____MODERN ISRAEL *Lily Edelman*   2.00
_____MODERN NUMEROLOGY *Morris C. Goodman*   2.00
_____MY WORLD OF ASTROLOGY *Sydney Omarr*   2.00
_____NATURE'S MEDICINES *Richard Lucas*   2.00
_____NEW APPROACHES TO SEX IN MARRIAGE *John E. Eichenlaub, M.D.*   2.00
_____NEW CARBOHYDRATE DIET COUNTER *Patti Lopez-Pereira*   1.00
_____NEW CONCEPTS OF HYPNOSIS *Bernard C. Gindes, M.D.*   2.00
_____NUMEROLOGY—ITS FACTS AND SECRETS *by Ariel Yvon Taylor*   2.00
_____1001 BRILLIANT WAYS TO CHECKMATE *Fred Reinfeld*   2.00
_____1001 WINNING CHESS SACRIFICES & COMBINATIONS *Fred Reinfeld*   2.00
_____ORIENTAL SECRETS OF GRACEFUL LIVING *Boye De Mente*   1.00
_____OUR JEWISH HERITAGE *Rabbi Alfred Wolf & Joseph Gaer*   2.00
_____PALMISTRY MADE EASY *Fred Gettings*   2.00
_____PALMISTRY MADE PRACTICAL *Elizabeth Daniels Squire*   2.00
_____PALMISTRY SECRETS REVEALED *Henry Frith*   2.00
_____PEYOTE STORY *Bernard Roseman*   1.00
_____PIGEONS: HOW TO RAISE AND TRAIN THEM *by William H. Allen, Jr.*   2.00
_____POST-HYPNOTIC INSTRUCTIONS *Arnold Furst*   2.00
      How to give post-hypnotic suggestions for therapeutic purposes.
_____PRACTICAL GUIDE TO BETTER CONCENTRATION *Melvin Powers*   2.00
_____PRACTICAL GUIDE TO PUBLIC SPEAKING *Maurice Forley*   2.00
_____PRACTICAL GUIDE TO SELF-HYPNOSIS *Melvin Powers*   2.00
_____PRACTICAL HYPNOTISM *Philip Magonet, M.D.*   1.00
_____PRACTICAL YOGA *Ernest Wood*   2.00
_____PRACTICE OF HYPNOTIC SUGGESTION *George C. Kingsbury, M.D.*   1.00
_____PSYCHEDELIC ECSTASY *William Marshall & Gilbert W. Taylor*   2.00
_____PSYCHO-CYBERNETICS *Maxwell Maltz, M.D.*   2.00
_____PSYCHOLOGY OF HANDWRITING *Nadya Olyanova*   2.00
_____PSYCHOSOMATIC GYNECOLOGY *William S. Kroger, M.D.*   10.00
_____ROMANCE OF HASSIDISM *Jacob S. Minkin*   2.50
_____SCIENTIFIC HYPNOTISM *Ralph Winn, Ph.D.*   1.00
_____SECRET OF BOWLING STRIKES *Dawson Taylor*   2.00

WILSHIRE
Self-Improvement
LIBRARY

____SECRET OF PERFECT PUTTING *Horton Smith & Dawson Taylor* **2.00**
____SECRET OF SECRETS *U. S. Andersen* **2.00**
____SECRETS OF HYPNOTISM *S. J. Van Pelt, M.D.* **2.00**
____SEEING INTO THE FUTURE *Harvey Day* **..00**
____SELF-CONFIDENCE THROUGH SELF-ANALYSIS *E. Oakley* 1.00
____SELF-HYPNOSIS Its Theory, Technique & Application *Melvin Powers* **2.00**
____SELF-HYPNOSIS A Conditioned-Response Technique *Laurance Sparks* **2.00**
____SERVICE OF THE HEART *Evelyn Garfiel*
    A Guide to the Jewish Prayer Book **2.50**
____7 DAYS TO FASTER READING *William S. Schaill* **2.00**
____SEW SIMPLY, SEW RIGHT *by Mini Rhea & F. Leighton* 2.00
____SEX & HUMAN BEHAVIOR BY NUMBERS *Alexandra Kayhle* 2.00
____SEX AND HYPNOSIS *L. T. Woodward, M.D.* **2.00**
____SEX WITHOUT GUILT *Albert Ellis, Ph.D.* **2.00**
____SEXUALLY ADEQUATE FEMALE *Frank S. Caprio, M.D.* 1.75
____SEXUALLY ADEQUATE MALE *Frank S. Caprio, M.D.* 1.75
____STAMP COLLECTING FOR BEGINNERS *by Burton Hobson* 2.00
____STAMP COLLECTING FOR FUN & PROFIT *Frank Cetin* 1.00
____STORY OF ISRAEL IN STAMPS *Maxim & Gabriel Shamir* 1.00
____STUDENT'S GUIDE TO BETTER GRADES *J. A. Rickard* **2.00**
____STUDENT'S GUIDE TO EFFICIENT STUDY *D. E. Jones* 1.00
____STUTTERING AND WHAT YOU CAN DO ABOUT IT *W. Johnson, Ph.D.* **2.00**
____SUCCESS-CYBERNETICS *U. S. Andersen* **2.00**
____TAROT *Mouni Sadhu* 2.00
____TAROT OF THE BOHEMIANS *Papus* 2.00
____10 DAYS TO A GREAT NEW LIFE *William E. Edwards* **2.00**
____THERAPY THROUGH HYPNOSIS *edited by Raphael H. Rhodes* 2.00
____THINK AND GROW RICH *Napoleon Hill* **2.00**
____THOUGHT DIAL *Sydney Omarr* **2.00**
____THREE MAGIC WORDS *U. S. Andersen* **2.00**
____TREASURY OF COMFORT *edited by Rabbi Sidney Greenberg* **2.00**
____TREASURY OF THE ART OF LIVING *edited by Rabbi S. Greenberg* 2.00
____VEGETARIAN COOKERY *Janet Walker* **2.00**
____WITCHCRAFT, MAGIC & OCCULTISM—A Fascinating History *W. B. Crow* 2.00
____WITCHCRAFT—THE SIXTH SENSE *Justine Glass* 2.00
____YOU ARE NOT THE TARGET *Laura Archera Huxley* **2.00**
____YOU CAN ANALYZE HANDWRITING *Robert Holder* **2.00**
____YOU CAN LEARN TO RELAX *Dr. Samuel Gutwirth* 1.00
____YOUR SUBCONSCIOUS POWER *Charles M. Simmons* **2.00**
____YOUR THOUGHTS CAN CHANGE YOUR LIFE *Donald Curtis* 2.00
____ZODIAC REVEALED *Rupert Gleadow* 2.00

NOTES

NOTES

NOTES